AF560255

Knowledgeable Culture

Knowledgeable Culture

Edited by
Dr. G. VISVANATHAN
Professor, Department of Education,
Annamalai University, Tamil Nadu
and
Dr.S.K.PANNEER SELVAM
Assistant Professor, Department of Education
Bharathidasan University, Tamil Nadu

RANDOM PUBLICATIONS
NEW DELHI (INDIA)

Knowledgeable Culture

ISBN 978-93-5111-354-6

Published in 2014 in India by

RANDOM PUBLICATIONS

4376-A/4B, Gali Murari Lal, Ansari Road
NewDelhi-110 002
Phone : +9111-43580356, 011-23289044
e-mail : sales@randompublications.com
info@randompublications.com

Type Setting by : Shah Computer Graphics, Delhi-110094
Printed at: Thomson Press (India) Ltd.

Contents

1
Social Maturity and Adjustment

4
Creativity and Social Maturity of Teacher Trainees

1. Social Maturity and Adjustment

1

Introduction

IMPORTANCE OF EDUCATION

Education is a social concept, which is philosophically evolved and physiologically developed. It has been accepted as a fundamental human right. Government has been taking on its shoulders the responsibility of providing Education to its citizens. National Plans have been giving larger outlays for Educational development as education is recognized as the investment human resources development.

The educators duty is not confined in giving instructions to the educand. He should mould the growing organism. The Kothari Commission reports states "The destiny of India is now being shaped in her Class Room" (1964-66) Hence the teacher plays an important role in shaping and molding the personality of the student.

SOCIAL MATURITY

Social maturity is the final expected outcome of social development and socialization. Psychologists list certain characteristics of social maturity. The socially mature person

(i) Is willing and able to orient himself in the various activities and customs of the group.

(ii) Is able to assume a reasonable amount of responsibility to adjust himself to the inevitable limitation and restrictions of the community life.

(iii) Can be original and yet conform to the broad pattern of his social environment.

(iv) Evaluates social problems from a purely selfish point of view but has regard to the rights and opinions of others.

(v) Accepts responsibility for his actions, does not indulge in self – purity.

(vi) Is relatively free from devastating emotions and is able to release his emotions in socially acceptable behaviour pattern.

(vii) Has a realistic level of aspiration and has a sound moral and social code that saves him from conflicts and feelings of guilt.

(viii) has many friends and contribute to social welfare

(ix) has a realistic self-concept, being conscious of his assets and limitations

(x) Is relatively secure and so open to experience which contribute to his continuous development.

In short, co-operation, pleasing manners, considerations for other positive and optimistic outlook on life and emotional maturity are signs of socially matured individuals.

Social maturity in the level of social development is characterized by independence from parental and adult control in social situation. It is characterized by the individual's ability to mix with people in social situations and manage social dealings without anybody's assistance. In other words, it is the attainment of the adult level social behaviour, after undergoing the natural process of socialization. (Lohithakshan, 2002)

Social maturity has been defined as "the growth and development of the individual, conditioned by both internal and external factors, which enable him to adapt himself'. The pattern of social maturity includes the following forms of behaviour group compatibility, kindness, and sympathy, efficiency, fair play, emotional adjustability, courtesy and politeness, self-confidence, co-operation, originality, curiosity, leadership and cheerfulness (pechstein and munn, 1939).

Today, in India, violent protects, agitations, strikes, bandhs and gheraos characterize our lives. The young people generally take a leading part in these activities and in creating unrest; they seem to be in revolt against society. As such, there is a deviation among people from social ideals, values and norms, which they cherish. Solution to this social moral degradation is value-oriented education. The chief aim of education is not merely the acquisition of knowledge but also the proper utilization of knowledge for the improvement of quality of human life. Social maturity can be operationally defined as social competence, shown in personal adequacy, interpersonal adequacy and social adequacy.

Social value places emphasis on concern for the well-being of human beings. The individual who is motivated by social value is sympathetic and will relate himself positively and constructively to other human beings. The six types of values are theoretical, economic, aesthetic, social, political and religious values, out of the large number of dimensions associated with the maturity.

ADJUSTMENT

Adjustment is a continuous process. According to Mouly (1968) adjustment is the process by means of which the individual seems to maintain physiological and psychological equilibrium and proper himself toward self-enhancement. It represents the quality of an individuals behaviour in relation to his interpersonal relations (Fredson, 1961) A well-adjusted person according to Chronbach (1954) is one who commits himself to socially desirable goals and uses his energies effectively in working towards them. He has a sense of security and a sense of belongingness. Adjustment is the process of establishing a satisfactory psychological relationship between the individual and his environment.

It is a process of constant interaction between the individuals and his environment. The adjustment is a deviant behaviour that goes beyond the limits of permissible behaviour established by the society. Such deviant behaviour, according to Lemert (1951) constitutes an individual or social problem.

The young students in our society undergo stormy period of life before they achieve full adulthood. Certain incidents in their life produces crises of adjustment and these incidents result in the breakdown of their normal life. Those who possess stable or consistent personality are considered as well adjusted. Lazarus (1976) is of the opinion that adjustment and personality are inextricably bound together.

An individual's ability to adopt himself to the environment is essential for his successful happy life. Studies have been reported in the literature, which emphasize the importance of desirable personality for better adjustment. Personality of an individual consists of his persistent tendency to make adjustment between his needs and environment.

The importance of personality adjustment is felt and recognized in all wakes of live. According to Patty and Johnson (1953), "a very general meaning of personality adjustment is the process of living itself, the dynamic equilibrium of the total organism of personality". Adjustment is an active process that occurs as the individual lives in his home, takes education, does some job and engages in social relationships. The important areas of personality adjustment are home and family adjustment, health adjustment, personal and emotional adjustment, educational adjustment, social and community adjustment and occupational adjustment.

The term adjustment has two meanings. In one sense, it is the process by which a person changes his behaviors to achieve a harmonious relation between himself and his environment and in the other; it is the state of such harmonious relationship. Adjustment consists of the psychological process by means of which the individual manages or copies with various demands. Webster's third new international dictionary gives as one of the definitions of adjustment "the effort to achieve a harmonious mental and behavioral balance between one's own personal needs and strivings and the demands of other individuals and of society". "adjustment refers to the way an individual gets along in satisfying the needs in an emotional, social and educational environment.

Essentially adjustment refers to the ability to satisfy the demands of one's surroundings as well as one's own needs. Originally, the meaning of adjustment was borrowed and changed from the concept of adaptation in biology, which refers to the biological changes that facilitate the survival a species. As long as the species was able to survive, adaptation was considered to be successful, regardless of how many individuals failed to adapt. At the psychological level, however adjustment has come to mean the individual's struggle to survive in his or her surroundings.

Until recently, adjustment involved a great deal of social conformity because in order to service socially, one had to become normal or like everyone else. In many ways, this notion reflected the relatively stable and widely accepted social order of society up to the 1950s. However, today in a word where everything including the social norms themselves, is changing successful adjustment calls for a more active role on the individual's part. Consequently, some psychologists are modifying the meaning of adjustment to include more of a two-way relationship between individuals and their surroundings.

According to Lazarus (1976), "the relationship which becomes established among the organism, the environment and the personality is adjustment. Adjustment involved realties the individuals most effectively to society, at the same time society provided the names of realizing the individual's potential for perceiving, feelings, thinking and creative activity including the changing of society itself. The practical implications of the present investigations are useful for the healthy development of the adolescents of all the research areas in the field of education adolescence appears to be the best-explored area. Adolescents are future pillars of the nations.

As R. Lazarus points out "actually adjustment consists of two kinds of processes, fittings oneself into given circumstances and fitting oneself into given circumstances and changing the circumstances to fit one's needs (Lazarus, 1976).

There are number of theories to explain the adjustment process. According to the theory of connectionism propounded by Thorndike, his famous laws of exercise and effect apply to the adjustment process in that a person tends to adjust to a situation or condition satisfactorily if he derives pleasure from it, behaviorism places emphasis on adjustment as an outcome of the effect upon the learner of environmental learning situation for the psychologists it reacting to the adjustment problem as an integrated whole.

NEED FOR THE PRESENT STUDY

Students are the backbone of the educational process. Education is a process and acts also as an instrument to bring out the innate behavior of the individual. The students of today are the youths of tomorrow and future citizens of the country, therefore proper development and growth of the students should be ensured even at the earliest age. The needful steps taken at this period ensures a healthy democracy in the country. Adjustment problems of higher secondary students have always attracted the attention of educational psychologists all over the globe. An educated person should be able to make effective adjustments with the environment were one is destined to live. Social development is continuous and cumulative. Adolescents are subjected to more worried and often more conflicts.

An adolescent is socially natured when there is progressive capacity, for looking after themselves and for participating in those activities, which need toward ultimate independence. Social maturity has three components viz., personal adequacy interpersonal adequacy and social adequacy. Social matured adolescent has no difficult in performing the roles and task expected of him and is relatively well adjusted. The present study is intended to study the relationships between the social maturity and adjustment of higher secondary school students.

STATEMENT OF THE PROBLEM

The above discussion has made the present investigator to choose the problem at hand and it is stated as follows: *"Social maturity and Adjustment of Higher Secondary school students of Nagappatinam District".*

OPERATIONAL DEFINITION OF THE TERMS

Social Maturity

Social Maturity is the progressive capacity to participate in activities, which help an individual to become independent.

Adjustment

Adjustment is the process by which an individual maintains a balance between his needs

Higher Secondary Students

Students who are studying first year Higher Secondary Schools in different group subjects.

OBJECTIVES OF THE STUDY

The following are the objectives for the present investigation.

1. To find out the social maturity of the Higher Secondary School students.
2. To find out if there is any significant difference in social maturity of students belonging to different sub samples. (Gender, Local, Type of school, parental education).
3. To find out the adjustment of Higher Secondary School Students.
4. To find out if there is any significant difference in the adjustment of students belonging to different sub samples (Gender, locale, Parental education, Type of School).
5. To find out whether there is any significant relationship between social maturity and adjustment scores.

HYPOTHESIS

The hypotheses of the study are as follows

1. The Social Maturity of the Higher Secondary School Students is high.
2. The Adjustment of the Higher Secondary School Students is high.
3. There is significant difference between the means of social maturity of Higher Secondary Students with regard to
   a. Gender (Male / Female)
   b. Locale (Rural / Urban)
   c. Parental Education (Literate / Illiterate)
   d. Type of School (Government / Private)
4. There is significant difference between the means of Adjustment of Higher Secondary with regard to
   a. Gender (Male / Female)
   b. Locale (Rural / Urban)
   c. Parental Education (Literate / Illiterate)
   d. Type of School (Government / Private)
5. There is significant relationship between social maturity and adjustment of Higher Secondary School Students of Nagappatinam District.

TOOLS OF THE STUDY

The following two tools have been used for the study.

Rao's social maturity scale (1998) and adjustment inventory for school students by Sinha, A.K.P. and Singh R.P (1984).

SAMPLE

Random sampling Technique was used in the selection of sample of 300 plus one Higher Secondary School Students in Nagappatinam District have been chosen of the areas of the population for studies. Out of 40 Higher Secondary School located in these areas 6 school were chosen by lottery method. Then from each of these six schools after having arranged the first year Higher

Secondary School Students belonging to different group in the alphabetical order, every fifth student was chosen to constitute the sample. Thus, from this six-selected school 300 plus one Higher Secondary School Students were selected for the sample.

DELIMITATION

This study has been confined only to the plus one Higher Secondary School Students of Nagappatinam District only.

A BRIEF RESUME OF THE SUCCEEDING CHAPTER

CHAPTER II Contains review of related studies. The methodology is given in CHAPTER III which contains the description of tools, samples and the statistical techniques used in this studies CHAPTER IV contains the analysis and interpretation of data with the discussion of results. The summary of the important finding and suggestion for further work and conclusion are given in CHAPTER V Bibliography follows and Appendices containing copies of the tools follow the bibliography.

2

Revie of Related Studies

INTRODUCTION

Review of related studies protects the investigator against unnecessary duplication, guides him in carrying out the investigation successfully, and familiarized him with research procedures.

SOCIAL MATURITY

Jyothi Chandra and Animesan (1993) study the mental ability and social maturity of the children of the integrated child development services and children of non ICDS. They concluded that the non ICDS group had scored significantly higher in the social maturity scale the ICDS group.

Lorrie A Shepard and Mary Lee Smith (1987) studied the effects of retention of Kindergarten students achievement and effective outcomes at the end of first grade. The study analyzed 40 Kindergarten students who had been retained at schools with a high retention rate. A control group of promoted students was established with children who matched on socioeconomic and achievement levels from schools that did not practice retention. Both groups were compared at the end of first grade on a number of outcome measures, including social maturity. The results of the study showed no different in social maturity between retained and promoted students at the end of the first grade.

Goseh A, Pankau R. (1994) studied the social emotional and behaviour adjustment in children with Williams – Beuren syndrome. Their study revealed that children with Williams – Beuren syndrome are social Immature and less adjusted socially then the control individuals.

Leslie Getzinger (2005) evaluated the New Maxico Kindergarten Plus program. Assessments show higher social maturity skills, greater parental involvement, and preliteracy gains. The first evaluation of the only Kindergarten Plus program in the nation demonstrated that the extra school time the program provides helps children flourish both socially and academically and also increases parental involvement in their children's education.

Stevan Richfield (2004) has prepared a social maturity strategy sheet. According to him many children do not mature at the same. Time to wide developmental discrepancies in early adolescence Middle School presents a melting pot of maturity levels, Many kids embrace the entrance into the fascinating cultural and social world that sets them apart from adults but part of teenage life. Thos chronological peers that remind them of their earlier immature selves are likely to be ridiculed and or rejected. Thus, the child who emotional lags in places in a puzzling position.

Getzels and Jackson (1962) have characterized the mature and moral person as perceiving and admitting to personal short comings, holding to personal ideals, transcending such qualities as appearance and social acceptability, "identifying with humanity beyond the immediate confines of his own groups". Research also shows that these abilities to predict social and personal consequences, to adapt to change, to become responsible and altruistic and to learn to transcend self can all be taught and developed through proper education.

Bandua and Walters (1963) report that the use of differential social reinforcement with modeling role-playing and directive verbalization have been found as effective instructional procedures in developing appropriate social behaviour.

Cooperrsmith's (1968) studies disclose that the person with good self-esteem is most likely to be an active, creative, socially aware capable and balanced person.

Proper teaching strategies or procedure have been found effective by Bryan and Walbeck (1971)l Rogers and Vasta (1970)l Staub (1971) and O'Connor (1971) in developing socially responsible.

Behaviour in Children

Maslow (1971) summarizes his research on the critical aspects of social and personal maturity; he concludes that education could help create the good and mature person by facilitating the development of positive consciousness through focusing on the enhancement of intrinsic values, Excellency, joy and peak qualities of good peak experiences.

Rosenthal (1973) has found that the qualities of good teacher models are then found to include the ability to be positive, accepting, perceptive, friendly, supportive, and "able to create to warmer social emotional mood around their students".

Rao (1978) has found that social maturity of children shows a positive and significant relationship with intelligence and self esteem. Girls generally score higher than boys do in social maturity. The children from private schools score more on social maturity than the children from government schools.

Saovaluk (1983) has found that the B.Ed college students with high social economic status background are found to be more socially matured than those coming from low social economic status. The students having dominant, high leadership radicalism and low neuroticism personality traits are more socially matured than those having submissive, low leadership, conventionalism and high neuroticism personality traits respectively.

Greenberger (1984) has found that two types of adolescent social relations are associated with autonomy: more and better family relations and a higher level of involvement in school, In addition, there is a strong association between academic achievement and social responsibility.

Asthana (1989) has found that social maturity among school going children has increased with increase in grade level, the growth rate being the highest in the first school year. Intelligence, age and academic achievement are significantly associated with the social maturity of children sex and social economic status are not found to contribute to social maturity of different grade levels.

Agnihotri (1991) has found that the social maturity is the social ingredient, psychological characteristics have influenced the social maturity of the children. Social maturity is independent of traditions of learning. Tribal are found to be only just aware of social norms while non-tribal affirm their consciousness of these norms. The tribal and non-tribal differ in terms of their placement on attributes of social maturity.

Mulia (1991) has observed that there is no significant difference in social maturity among higher secondary students of the three streams arts, commerce and science and between the two sexes.

Hemantha Kumar (2003) has found that the factors of social isolation, a dimension of social maturity, is found to be affected the problems of adolescent girls in such as a way that the girls with a higher degree of social isolation are found to face more intensity of the problems than those with lesser degree of social isolation. Thus, social isolation is positively related to the problems of adolescent girls.

ADJUSTMENT

According to **K.V. Smith and W.H. Smith (1958)** the well – adjusted person experienced conflicts and attacks his problems in a realistic manner. His organic emotional and social need is fully satisfied. He does not suffer from emotional craving and social isolation.

Rajamanickam and Mercy Arunmozhi (1992) have studied the adjustment problems of adolescent girls in relation to psychosomatic disorders. The study revealed that there is a positive association between adjustment problems and psychosomatic disorders in the case of adolescent girls. The well adjusted girls were emotionally stable and least prone to psychosomatic disorders. Girls from affluent families were well adjusted and had the least psychosomatic disorders where as the girls from poor families had more adjustment problem and psychosomatic disorders. Girls from forward communities were well adjusted and free from psychosomatic disorders while the girls from backward and schedule caste communities had more adjustment problems and prone to more psychosomatic disorders.

Family background and school adjustment problems was studied by **Lortan et at (1977)** Their experiments show that subjects from rejecting parents had more serious aggressive problems that the subjects from over protective parents.

Prince and Rajamanickam (1987) studied the adjustment problems of sports school boys in Tamil Nadu. Their study revealed the following findings (i) the urban and rural school students were better adjusted than the sports schools students (ii) rural school students were found to be emotionally unstable than the semi urban sports school students (iii) the urban sports students were emotionally unstable than the rural and semi urban sports school students.

Boyscin (1957) investigated the adjustment problems Negro students and found that approximately 20-25 percent were poor in the areas of home, social, health and emotional adjustment, according to London (1957) racial segregation hinders social adjustment of Americans because it is in direct violation of fundamental Americal ideals, causing moral conflict among the while population, Pirece Jones and his associates (1959) examined adolescents racial and ethnic differences in social attitudes and adjustment. They found that a negative orientation to society was stronger is young Negroes next most evident in young Maxican Americans and understandably least pronounced in white youth.

According to **Claveason (1966)** a morally healthy, individual maintain good adjustment with social instructions.

Gates (1936) found significant relationship between scholarships and social adjustment. According to him failure in school work leads to social mal-adjustment, But Eckert (1935) Meel and Mathew (1935) and Gough (1949) found that over achievers tended to be rather withdrawn in social relations, Young (1939) found a significant relationship between social adjustment and achievement, But young Drought and Bergstreser (1937) found no relationship between social adjustment and achievement. Steinzerr (1944) and Kuntz and Swenson (1951) found that over achievers were better able than the average students in their social adjustment.

Rangari Ashok (1987) administered the adjustment inventory to 1220 scheduled caste and 120 non-scheduled caste junior college students to explore caste differences in adjustment. Results indicate that the adjustment of non-scheduled casts in home and family, Social, personal, emotional, educational and health areas was superior to that of scheduled castes.

Rajamanickam and Prince Jayakumar (1987) made an attempt to study the adjustment problems of sports and school boys in Tamil Nadu. The sample consisted of 255 sports school boys drawn from three sports schools of Tamil Nadu. An adjustment inventory for school students was administered. Results showed that the rural sports school students were better adjusted than urban students. No significant difference in adjustment was found between semi-urban and rural sports school stations.

Sanmugaganesan (1996) conducted a study among 480 university students to find out the effect of anxiety of adjustment and achievement. Anxiety scale, adjustment inventory for college students socio-economic status scale was used. The results showed that professional students from urban and rural areas do not differ in the adjustment.

Rangari Ashok (1987) administered the adjustment inventory to 120 scheduled caste and 120 non schedule caste junior college students to explore caste difference in adjustment. Results indicate that the adjustment of non-scheduled castes in home and family, social, personal, emotional, educational and health areas was superior to that of scheduled castes.

Rajamanickam and Prince Jayakumar (1987) made an attempt to study the adjustment problems of sports school boys in Tamil Nadu. The sample consisted of 255 sports school boys drawn from three sports of Tamil Nadu. An adjustment inventory for school students was administered. Results showed that the rural sports school students were better adjusted than urban students. No significant difference in adjustment was found between semi urban and rural sports school stations.

Rao (1972) and Bhagia (1966) found a positive relationship between pupils adjustment scores and scores on achievement. Rao (1972) also found that persons having neurotic difficulties were observed to be poor in adjustment to academic situations and performed unsatisfactorily. Resnick (1951) found out that pupils earning high grades also made high scores on adjustments indicating a more satisfactory personal adjustment.

Congdon (1943) Houston and Marzolt (1944) Hibler and Larson (1944), Carroli and James (1941) have found several adjustment problems to be associated with under achievement Stienze (1944), Cattell (1945) and Thompson (1948) pointed out that over achievers were characterized by good adjustment to school and general awareness and responsiveness to environments influences.

According to **Stromswold** and **Wren (1948)** a well adjusted student exhibits high intrinsic interest in the subject matter of study, positive attitude towards the curriculum stability of his grades, balanced emotional life, ability to concentrate for a reasonable length of time on and ability to enjoy life in many areas French (1958) concluded that lack of adjustment to success, Frankel (1962) found over achievers too be more adequately adjusted to the academic situation.

The studies conducted by **Rajamanickam and Vasanthal (1993)** revealed that there is a positive association between adolescent students adjustment scores and their scores. Parents higher educational levels had positive effects on students adjustment problems and achievement.

The high achievers (Gillmore 1977) have been found to be characterized by a strong, warm and empathic relationship between parents and children. On the other hand the under achievers family environment (Morrow and Wilson 1977) has been found to be quite different from that of the high achievers. Studies of Anderson (1968) Curry (1962) Myres (1966) revealed that higher SES has positive influence upon the scholastic achievement of students. Jain (1965) also reported negligible relationship between adjustment and achievement. Mittle (1962) Chawla and Pandey (1962) found positive relationship between adjustment and achievement.

Adjustment problems of Higher secondary students have attracted the attention of educational psychologists all over the globe. Gupta (1978) found positive and significant relationship between personality adjustment and extroversion introversion. Neuroticism was found to be highly significant relationship between personality adjustment and extroversion introversion. Neuroticism was found to be highly significant. Adjustment studies made by Sherman and Joa (1942) clearly indicate that neurotics have lower frustration tolerance. According to them introverts and neurotics have more adjustment problems than others.

Chaudhary Binay, et.al (1992) examined the effects of extraversion and neuroticism on adjustment in 4 different areas of adjustment (home, health, social and emotional) among 100 college students. The tools were Eysenck Personality Inventory and the Bell adjustment inventory the same was grouped as high and low in extrovert and neuroticism. High and low extroverts did not differ significantly in home. Healthy and emotional adjustment. However, high and low extroverts differed significantly in social adjustment. High and low neurotic subjects differed significantly in all the four area of adjustments. Low Neurotic subjects were better adjusted than high neurotic subjects.

Vinitha (1993) investigated the relationship between academic anxiety and adjustment among 200 female high school students (aged 14-17 years) using the Bell's adjustment inventory and academic scale for children. It was hypothesized that the greater the academic anxiety, the greater was the maladjustment. Subjects were categorized into two groups, the high anxiety group and low anxiety group. The mean values of different areas of adjustment 142 healthy social and emotional and over all adjustment were higher in greater anxiety, group, as compared with low anxiety group indicating anxiety leads to poor adjustment.

Musser (1969) points out that no other factor exerts more influences on one's over behaviour, the emotional reactions, the cognitive functions, the covert attitudes and the general psychological adjustment than one's sex.

Ashok Rangari (1986) studied the personality adjustment of male and female college students on five adjustment areas viz., home and family, social, personal and emotional, education and health. The sample consisted of 102 male and 102 female students matched for age, educational and area of residence, Palson adjustment inventory (1977) was administered. The results showed significant difference in all these four areas. The girls were found to have better adjustment than boys.

Chaldha and Chandra (1985) have made a comparative study of the adolescent boys and girls in relation school adjustment and academic achievement. The study revealed that (i) Adjustment of an adolescent affects scholastic achievement (ii) Better emotional and educational adjustment help to achieve more in the school (iii) Social adjustment does not affect scholastic achievement (iv) Adolescent boys have better adjustment than adolescent girls emotional and educational adjustment are better among boys. There are no differences between boys and girls in social adjustment.

Sundararajan and Anjanyalu (1993) found no significant difference between boys and girls in their total adjustment.

Brar (1973) studied the adjustment problems of higher secondary students. According to him, adjustment problems were not so prominent among the girls.

Jayaraman (1996) studied the adjustment problems of higher secondary students in relation to some selected variables. According to him, adjustment problems of boys and girls varied significantly.

Deutsch (1960) found that the Begro girls excelled the Negro boy in personal and social adjustment. Hall and Gentry (1962) indicated that Negro male students had made a better adjustment, or had been fully accepted in the integrated school than the Negro female students. Musgrove and Whitesides (1973) carried out the study of Negro and White low socio –economic class children. Smith (1961) found that there were no rural- urban differences in personal and social adjustment of Negro children in South America.

Brar (1973) studied a sample of Adivasi and Non-Adivasi adolescents selected from ninth, tenth, and eleventh standards, from hoshangabad area. Results show that problem of social adjustment was acute among Adivasi subjects. The findings of Ghorpade's (1978) survey of the mental maladjustment among the college students of Bombay university reveal that about twenty six percent of the youth, or approximately every fourth student of the Bombay University had either a mild or severe problem of adjustment, the female students show considerably high incidence of both mild and severe forms of maladjustment and linguistic sub – culture and social class of the student seem to be the important factors contributing to the maladjustment of various type Rangari (1984) was investigated into the personality adjustment of college students from senior colleges of Aurangabad in Maharashtra State. He found that the urban women were found to be better than urban men on personal and emotional adjustment; and women from rural area were found to be better on health adjustment; and women from rural areas were found to be better on health adjustment than their men counterparts. Sarasulat et al studied the students from Higher Secondary schools of Delhi and found that girls were better adjusted as compared to boys on health, social, school and total adjustment. The female students as compared to the male students tended to be better in home and family adjustment, personal and emotional adjustment and educational adjustment even though both the groups were matched in age, education and area of residence.

Hicks (1934) Natraj (1968) Pathak (1970) and **Chadha** and **Chandra (1985)** found significant differences between boys and girls on adjustment. It shows that during the stormy period of adolescence girls compared to boys feel more in conflict, more anxious and more helpless.

CONCLUSION

Thus the view of studies related to this area of investigation enabled the present investigator to plan this course of research and in the formulation of suitable hypotheses for this study. The description of the tools, the sample and the statistical techniques used in this study are given in chapter III.

3

Methodology

INTRODUCTION

The present investigation has been undertaken with a view to find out the following

1. The social maturity of the higher secondary school students of Nagappatinam District.
2. If there is any significant difference in the social maturity belonging to different sub samples (Gender, locale, Type of school, parental education).
3. The adjustment of the higher secondary school students of Nagappatinam district.
4. If there is any significant difference in the Adjustment of students belonging to different sub samples (Gender, locale, type of school, Parental education).
5. Whether there is any significant relationship between social maturity and adjustment scores.

In order to realize the above objectives two tools namely Rao's Social Maturity Scale (1998) and Sinha and Singh's Adjustment inventory (1984) were administrated to the selected sample of 300 plus one higher secondary school students.

SOCIAL MATURITY SCALE

In order to measure Social maturity of the 300 first Higher Secondary students 'Social Maturity' scale were administered. The social maturity scale by Rao (1998) has been used to measure the social maturity of higher secondary students. It includes 90 items. 4 alternative answers are given for each statement. The subjects were asked to put tick mark to the statement that suits him the most. Each item has 4 responses –viz, Strongly agree; Agree, Disagree, strongly disagree. For favouable statement, the 'Strongly agree' response was give a weight of 4, the 'Agree' response was given a weight of 3, the 'Disagree' response was given a weight of 2 and the 'strongly disagree' response a weight of 1. For unfavourable statements, the scoring system was reversed with Strongly disagree response being given the 4 weight and the 'strongly agree' response a weight of 1. The sum of the items credits represented the individual's total score. Experts in the field of psychology and education ascertained the face validity of the scale.

RELIABILITY

Split – half method, test and retest and internal consistency method was applied for obtaining the reliability co-efficient of this scale. It was found to be 0.74.

VALIDITY

Experts in the field of psychology and education have ascertained the face validity of the tool.

ADJUSTMENT INVENTORY

The adjustment inventory for the school students constructed and standardized by Sinha and Singh (1984) has been used in this study.

It is a self administered inventory. The adjustment inventory has 60 items. Subjects are asked to read the questions carefully and then put a tick mark on the cell below either 'yes' or 'no' for scoring, each correct answer is to be assigned a score of 1 and an incorrect answer a score of Zero. There are two types of items positive items and negative items. All the positive items that endorsed by the pupils or subjects as 'yes' and all negative items that are endorsed by the subjects are 'no' are given a score of 1. A score of zero is awarded to other answers.

RELIABILITY

Split – half method, test and retest and internal consistency method was applied for obtaining the reliability co-efficient of the scale. It was found to be 0.78.

VALIDITY

Experts in the field of psychology and education have ascertained the face validity of the tool.

SAMPLE

Random sampling Technique was used in the selection of sample of 300 plus one Higher Secondary School Students in Nagappatinam district. Out of 40 higher secondary school located in Nagappatinam district 6 school chosen by lottery method. Then from each of these six schools after having arranged the plus one students belonging to different group in the alphabetical order, every fifty student was chosen to constitute the sample. Thus from these six selected school, 300 plus one higher secondary school students were selected for the sample.

THE STATISTICAL TECHNIQUES USED

The means and standard deviations for the sample, and its sub samples are computed for Social maturity and Adjustment scores

The test of significances (t-test) was used in order to the find out the significance of means of pairs of sub sample in respect of their Social Maturity and Adjustment.

The person's product moment 'r' was computed between the social maturity and Adjustment scores.

The means of the Social Maturity and Adjustment scores are represented through histogram at the appropriate places.

CONCLUSION

Thus all two tools namely social maturity and adjustment scale were administered to the same sample of 300 plus one Higher Secondary school students and the obtained data was statistically treated and interpreted. They are presented in the succeeding chapter.

4

The Analysis and Interpretations of Data

INTRODUCTION

It may be recalled that the present investigation is intended to find out

(i) The social maturity of plus one higher secondary school students in Nagappatinam District.

(ii) If there is any significant difference in the social maturity of plus one higher secondary school students belonging to different sub-samples.

(iii) The adjustment of plus one higher secondary school students.

(iv) If there is any significant difference in the adjustment of plus one higher secondary school students belonging to different sub samples and

(v) If there is any significant relationship exists between social maturity and adjustment.

In order to realize the above objectives it may be recalled that the copies of social maturity scale and adjustment inventory was administered to the sample of 300 plus one higher secondary students studying in the schools of Nagappatinam District, Tamil Nadu. The scores of the subjects for social maturity and adjustment were found out and subjected to statistical analysis.

STATISTICAL ANALYSIS AND INTERPRETATION OF THE DATA

The mean and standard deviation of the social maturity and adjustment scores for the entire sample was calculated. They are given in the table 1 that the plus one higher secondary students have shown high social maturity and adjustment.

The mean and standard deviation of the total group are 232.68 and 22.82 respectively. It may be remembered that a student can get a maximum score of 360. Since the mean value is greater than the mid. The mean and standard deviation of the total group are 232.68 core 180 social maturity of higher secondary students is high. The mean social maturity scores of all the sub-sample are found to be greater than 180. Hence it can be concluded that social maturity of higher secondary students is high.

The mean and standard deviation of the total group of adjustment scores are 19.47 and 8.36. The student can get a maximum score of 60. In this scale low score indicate better adjustment. Since the mean score is 19.47 the adjustment of the student is high.

Table 1

The Means and standard Deviations of the Social Maturity and Adjustment of the Entire sample

Entire Sample	N	Mean	S.D.
Social Maturity	300	232.68	22.82
Adjustment		19.47	08.36

The means and standard deviation of the social maturity scores for the sub samples are calculated and then they are given in the following tables (Tables 2, 3, 4, 5)

Table 2

The Mean and Standard Deviations of the Social Maturity Scores of the Male and Female Plus one Higher Secondary School Students

Sub Samples	N	Mean	S.D.
Male	150	232.77	19.99
Female	150	232.76	25.62

The means and standard deviation of the social maturity scores of male and female students were calculated. They are given in the above table. It is seen from the table 2 that the means of Male and Female plus one students of Social Maturity is more or less same.

Table 3

The Mean and Standard Deviations of the Social Maturity Scores of the Rural and Urban Plus one Higher Secondary School Students

Sub Samples	N	Mean	S.D.
Rural	150	234.84	23.61
Urban	150	230.69	22.13

The means and standard deviation of the social maturity adjustment students were calculated. They are given in the above table. It is seen from the table that the mean of the social maturity scores of the rural plus one students is higher than the mean of the Urban school students.

Table 4

The Mean and Standard Deviations of the Social Maturity Scores of Students of Literate Parents and Illiterate Parents

Sub Samples	N	Mean	S.D.
Students of Literate Parents	193	233.56	23.34
Students of Illiterate Parents	107	231.35	22.25

The means and standard deviation of the social maturity scores of students of literate and illiterate parents were calculated. They are given in the above table. It is seen from the table 4 that the mean of the social maturity scores students of literate parents is higher than the mean of the students of illiterate parents.

Table 5

The Mean and Standard Deviations of the Social Maturity Scores of the Plus One Higher Secondary School Students studying in Government Schools and Private School

Sub Samples	N	Mean	S.D.
Government School Students	150	235.24	24.16
Private School Students	150	230.30	21.45

The means and standard deviation of the social maturity scores of government and private school students were calculated. They are given in the above table. It is seen from the table 5 that the mean of the social Maturity scores of Government school students are shown higher than the mean of the private school students.

Table 6

The Mean and Standard Deviations of the Adjustment Scores of the Male and Female plus one Higher Secondary School Students

Sub Samples	N	Mean	S.D.
Male	150	19.85	8.19
Female	150	19.25	8.60

The means and standard deviation of Adjustment scores of male and female students were calculated. They are given in the above table. It is seen from the table 6 that the means of Male and Female plus on students of adjustment is more or less same.

Table 7

The Mean and Standard Deviations of the Adjustment Scores of the Rural and Urban plus one Higher Secondary School Students

Sub Samples	N	Mean	S.D.
Rural	150	19.41	8.34
Urban	150	19.70	8.47

The means and standard deviation of Adjustment scores of rural and urban students were calculated is seen from the table 7. That the mean of the adjustment scores of the rural and urban plus one students is more or less same.

Table 8

The Mean and Standard Deviations of the Adjustment Scores of Students of Literate parents and Illiterate Parents

Sub Samples	N	Mean	S.D.
Students of Literate Parents	193	20.34	8.41
Students of illiterate parents	150	19.70	8.47

The means and standard deviation of Adjustment scores of students of literate and illiterate parents students were calculated. It is seen from the table 8 that the mean of the adjustment scores students of literate parents is higher than the mean of the students of illiterate parents.

Table 9

The Mean and Standard Deviations of the Adjustment Scores of the plus one Higher Secondary School Students studying in Government Schools and Private School

Sub Samples	N	Mean	S.D.
Government School Students	150	18.51	8.24
Private School Students	150	20.59	8.44

The means and standard deviation of Adjustment scores of Government and private school students were calculated. It is seen from the table 9 that the mean of the adjustment scores of private school students are shown higher than the mean of the Government School Students.

NULL HYPOTHESIS 1

There is no significant difference between the means of social maturity scores of male and female students

TABLE 10

The mean and Standard Deviation and Cr of the social maturity scores of the Male and Female plus one Higher Secondary School Students.

Sub Samples	N	Mean	S.D.	C.R.	Level of Significance (0.05)
Male	150	232.77	19.99	0.33	Not significant
Female	150	232.76	25.62		

The details of the calculation is given in the table (10) The CR values is found to be .003, which is not significant at 0.05 levels. Therefore the null hypothesis is retained and it is concluded that there is no significant difference between the male and female plus one, higher secondary school students in respect of their social maturity. Thus the study shows that the gender cannot cause any significant difference to the plus one higher secondary school student's social maturity.

NULL HYPOTHESIS 2

There is no significant difference between the means of social maturity scores of Rural and Urban School Students

TABLE 11

The mean and Standard Deviation and Cr of the social maturity scores of the Rural and Urban plus one Higher Secondary School Students.

Sub Samples	N	Mean	S.D.	C.R.	Level of Significance (0.05)
Rural	150	234.84	23.61	1.572	Not significant
Urban	150	30.69	22.13		

The details of the calculation is given in the table (11) The CR values is found to be 1.572, which is not significant at 0.05 levels. Therefore the null hypothesis is retained and it is concluded that there is no significant difference between the rural and urban plus one, higher secondary school students in respect of their social maturity.

Thus the study shows that the locality cannot cause any significant difference to the plus one higher secondary school student's social maturity.

NULL HYPOTHESIS 3

There is no significant difference between the means of social maturity scores of Rural and Urban School Students

TABLE 12

The mean and Standard Deviation and Cr of the social maturity scores of the Students of Literate Parents and illiterate Parents

Sub Samples	N	Mean	S.D.	C.R.	Level of Significance (0.05)
Students of literate parents	193	233.56	23.34	.811	Not significant
Students of illiterate parents	107	231.35	22.15		

The details of the calculation is given in the table (12) The CR values is found to be 0.811, which is not significant at 0.05 levels. Therefore the null hypothesis is retained and it is concluded that there is no significant difference between the plus one, higher secondary school students who have illiterate and literate parents in respect of their social maturity.

Thus the study shows that the parental education cannot causes any significant difference to the plus one higher secondary school student's social maturity.

NULL HYPOTHESIS 4

There is no significant difference between the means of social maturity scores of Government and Private Students

TABLE 13

The mean and Standard Deviation and Cr of the social maturity scores of the plus one higher secondary school students studying in government schools and private School.

Sub Samples	N	Mean	S.D.	C.R.	Level of Significance (0.05)
Government School Students	150	235.24	24.16	1.873	Not significant
Private School Students	150	230.30	21.45		

The details of the calculation is given in the table (13) The CR values is found to be 1.873, which is not significant at 0.05 levels. Therefore the null hypothesis is retained and it is concluded that there is no significant difference between the Government and Private plus one, higher secondary school students in respect of their social maturity.

Thus the study shows that the Type of School cannot cause any significant difference to the plus one higher secondary school student's social maturity.

NULL HYPOTHESIS 5

There is no significant difference between the means of social maturity scores of Male and Female Students

TABLE 14

The mean and Standard Deviation and Cr of the Adjustment Scores of the Male and Female plus one higher secondary school students

Sub Samples	N	Mean	S.D.	C.R.	Level of Significance (0.05)
Male	150	19.85	8.19	.619	Not significant
Female	150	19.25	8.60		

The details of the calculation is given in the table (14) The CR values is found to be 0.619, which is not significant at 0.05 levels.

Therefore the null hypothesis is retained and it is concluded that there is no significant difference between the male and female plus one, higher secondary school students in respect of their adjustment.

Thus the study shows that the gender cannot cause any significant difference to the plus one higher secondary school student's adjustment.

NULL HYPOTHESIS 6

There is no significant difference between the means of adjustment scores of Rural and Urban School Students

TABLE 15

The mean and Standard Deviation and Cr of the adjustment scores of the Rural and Urban plus one Higher Secondary School Students.

Sub Samples	N	Mean	S.D.	C.R.	Level of Significance (0.05)
Rural	150	19.41	8.34	-0.302	Not significant
Urban	150	19.70	8.47		

The details of the calculation is given in the table (15) The CR values is found to be -0.302, which is not significant at 0.05 levels. Therefore the null hypothesis is retained and it is concluded that there is no significant difference between the rural and urban plus one, higher secondary school students in respect of their adjustment.

Thus the study shows that the locality cannot cause any significant difference to the plus one higher secondary school student's adjustment.

NULL HYPOTHESIS 7

There is no significant difference between the means of adjustment scores of Rural and Urban School Students

TABLE 16

The mean and Standard Deviation and Cr of the social maturity scores of the Students of Literate Parents and illiterate Parents

Sub Samples	N	Mean	S.D.	C.R.	Level of Significance (0.05)
Students of literate parents	193	20.34	8.41	2.215	Significant
Students of illiterate parents	107	18.13	8.21		

The details of the calculation is given in the table (16) The CR values is found to be 2.215, which is significant at 0.05 levels. Therefore the null hypothesis is rejected and it is concluded that there is no significant difference between the plus one, higher secondary school students who have illiterate and literate parents in respect of their adjustment.

Thus the study shows that the parental education cannot causes any significant difference to the plus one higher secondary school student's adjustment

NULL HYPOTHESIS 8

There is no significant difference between the means of adjustment scores of Government and Private Students

TABLE 17

The mean and Standard Deviation and Cr of the adjustment scores of the plus one higher secondary school students studying in government schools and private School.

Sub Samples	N	Mean	S.D.	C.R.	Level of Significance (0.05)
Government School Students	150	18.51	8.24	- 2.160	Not significant
Private School Students	150	20.59	8.44		

The details of the calculation is given in the table (17) The CR values is found to be – 2.160, which is not significant at 0.05 levels. Therefore the null hypothesis is retained and it is concluded that there is no significant difference between the Government and Private plus one, higher secondary school students in respect of their adjustment.

Thus the study shows that the Type of School cannot cause any significant difference to the plus one higher secondary school student's adjustment.

NULL HYPOTHESIS 9

There is no significant relationship between the social maturity and adjustment scores of higher secondary school students.

TABLE 18

Correlation Co-Efficient ("R") Between the Social Maturity and Adjustment

Sub Samples	Mean	S.D.	df	'r'	Level of Significance (0.05)
Social Maturity and Adjustment	232.68 0.84	22.82 0.05	298	19.47	8.36

It is seen from the table 18 that the correlation co-efficient value is found to be .084 there which is not significant at the 0.05 level. Thus there is no evidence in the present study to show that they are significantly related.

Discussion of the results

It has been found in the present study the social maturity of higher secondary school students in Nagappatinam District are high and some sub samples differ in their social maturity.

It has been found in the present study the adjustment of higher secondary school students in Nagappatinam District are high and some sub samples differ in their adjustment. There is positive correlation found out between social maturity and adjustment.

CONCLUSION

Thus the analysis of the data generated by the administration of the tools to a sample of 300 plus one higher secondary school students are summarized in the succeeding chapter

5

The Important Findings, Suggestions for Future Work and Conclusion

INTRODUCTION

The two tools namely the social maturity scale and adjustment inventory were administered to the 300 plus one higher secondary school students in Nagappatinam District with view to find out:

1. The social maturity of the higher secondary school students.
2. If there is any significant difference in social maturity of student belonging to different sub samples (Gender, Locale, Type of School, Parental education).
3. The adjustment of higher secondary school students.
4. If there is any significant difference in the adjustment of students belonging to different sub samples (Gender, Locale, Type of School, Parental education).
5. Whether there is any significant relationship between social maturity and adjustment.

The data generated from the above were statistically treated and the results that have yielded are presented in the succeeding paragraphs.

IMPORTANT FINDINGS

1. The social maturity of higher secondary school students is high.
2. The social maturity of male and female of higher secondary school students is high.
3. The rural and urban higher secondary school students are having high social maturity.
4. The students of literate parents and illiterate parents are having high social maturity.
5. The social maturity of government and private higher secondary school students is high.
6. The adjustment of the Higher Secondary School Students is high.
7. The adjustment of male and female of higher secondary school students is high.
8. The rural and urban higher secondary school students are having high adjustment.
9. The students of literate parents and illiterate parents are having high adjustment.
10. The adjustment of government and private higher secondary school students is high.
11. The male and female of higher secondary school students do not differ significantly in their social maturity.
12. The rural and urban school students do not differ significantly in their social maturity.
13. The Government and Private school students do not differ significantly in their social maturity.
14. The literate and illiterate parents of higher secondary school students do not differ significantly in their social maturity.
15. The male and female higher secondary school students do not differ significantly in their adjustment.
16. The rural and urban school students do not differ significantly in their adjustment.
17. The Government and Private school students do not differ significantly in their adjustment.

18. The literate and illiterate parents of higher secondary school students do not differ significantly in their adjustment..
19. There is a positive correlation between the social maturity and adjustment scores of higher secondary school students.

RECOMMENDATION

1. Improving the total climate of the schools to influence the values like social justice and quality.
2. Value education subjects may be introduced in the higher secondary syllabus.
3. Students should be encouraged to involve themselves not only in curricular activities but also in co-curricular and extracurricular activities.
4. Curriculum should contain ethical principles, codes of conduct, personal and inter personal virtues.

SUGGESTIONS FOR FUTURE RESEARCH

A replica the present study could be under taken at various parts of Tamil Nadu.

1. The social maturity and their academic achievement of higher secondary school students may be studied.
2. The same study could be conducted among college students.
3. A similar study may be undertaken at university level.
4. A comparative study may be made on social maturity and adjustment of Tamil Nadu Students and Kerala students.
5. A Study could be conducted on adjustment and their academic achievement of higher secondary school students may be studied.

CONCLUSION

Thus the present investigation has yielded many interesting results that are bound to add to the volume of knowledge already present in this field of investigation

BIBLIOGRAPHY

1. **Asthana, Anju: A** study of social maturity among school going children in the city of Luck now, P.hd., Education, university of Lucknow, 1989.
2. **Ashok Ranger, "**An investigation in to adjustment of college students in Marthwada" Psychological studies Vol.3 (1). 1986.
3. **Bhagta, M.M.** "Study of problem of school adjustment and developing an adjustment inventory", Doctoral Dissertation of Education, MSU, 1966.
4. **Brar, I.S**. "The adjustment problem faced byn the Higher Secondary school students" Journal of Educational Research and Extension (Vol. 914), page 202-208.1973.
5. **Chadha Jyoth and Animasen** "Mental ability and social maturity of the children of integrated child development services and the children of non- ICDS". Journal of community guidance and research, Vol 10, no.1, pp 47-58. 1993.
6. **Chandha, N.K. and Chandra** "A comparative study of the adolescent boys and girls in relation to third attitudes towards school adjustment and scholastic achievement". The Indian Journal of community Guidance Service Vol. 2, No.3 Sep.1985.
7. **Chaudhary, Binar, K and Singh, Ram B.,** "A study of adjustment in relation to some personality factors". Indian Journal of Psychometric and Education, Vol. 23(1), 33-36. 1992.
8. **Gates, A.I.** "Failure in reading and social mal-adjustment". Journal of National Education Association, 25, P-205-216-1936.
9. **Gosch A, Pankau R.** "Social-Emotional behavioural adjustment in children: with Williams – Beuren Syndrome. Am J Med Genet, 1994 Dec.1: 53 (4): 335-9. – 1994.
10. **Gupta, B.P.** "A study of personality adjustment in relation to intelligence sex, socio economic background and

personality dimensions of extraversion and Neuroticism", Ph.D., Thesis Utkal University 1978.

11. **Hicks** Adjustment of men and Women, Dissertation Abstract International 24, 21-22 1934.
12. **Jenkin N,** "Size constancy as a frustration of personal Adjustment and disposition" Journal of Abnormal and Social Psychology Vol, 5. 334-338.1958.
13. **Joseph Alexander E.,** and Rajamanickam, M. "A study of Adjustment problem among university students", Indian Journal of community guidance service, Vol. 5(1) 19-32. (1888).
14. **Lemert, E.M.,** Social Psychology, New York, McGraw Hill Book Co., Inc., 1981.
15. **Lortan, eal,** "Family background characteristics and social adjustment problems" – journal of community psychology Vol 5 (2) pp 142-148.
16. **Mital and Chaula,.** "Relation & Adjustment and achievement", Psychological studies No.2 pp 58-63. 1970.
17. **Mussen Personality R.** Abramson, Ed New York, Holt Rine Hart and Winston, 1969.
18. **Nataraj K,** "The adjustment of adolescent college girls", Psychological studies, Vol. 52 (7), 4 1968 2-43.
19. **Palsame M.N.** "Students adjustment at the university stage". Journal of Education and Psychology, Vol. 27(4), 321-332 1976.
20. **Pandy, A** "Adjustment between brig-ht and average students", Indian Educational Review, Vol 12 (4) PP 86-90, 1977.
21. **Pathak R.** "Sex difference among school children in the area of adjustment "Psychological Studies" (No.2) 54-56 1970.
22. **Prothox S,** "Children attitude towards school, their sex and mother's authoritanism", International Journal of sociology of familyl Vol.7 P140 1977.
23. **Rajamanickam and Prince Jayakumar** "Adjustment problems of sports school boys in Tamil Nadu", Indian Journal of community guidance service Vol 4 (2) (1987).

24. **Rajamanickam, M. and R.Mercy Arunmozhi (1992)** "Adjustment problem in relation to Psychometric disorders among the adolescent girls, "Journal of community Guidance and Research, Vol 9, No.2, PP 151-179.

25. **Rajamanickam, M. and R.Vasanthi (1993)** "Adjustment problems of adolescent students in relation to their achievement" Journal of Community Guidance and Research, Vol,. 10 No.3, PP 153-183.

26. **Rajkumar, S. "**Adjustment of Adolescents" Indian Educational Review Vol.XXI, 4, P.110 (1985).

27. **Rangari, Ashok** "Differences in adjustment of scheduled caste and non-scheduled caste students", Indian Psychologist, Vol, 4(2) 59-64.

28. **Rao N.** (1) "A progressive study of achievement in relation to academic adjustment", Indian Psychological abstract, Vol (5) September - October 1972.

29. **Resnick.** J. "A study of some relationship between high school grades and certain aspects of adjustment" Journal of Educational Research, Vol. 44 PP 321 - 3440 11951.

30. **Rosenweis, S.** An outline of Frustration theory, In Hunt, J.Me.V. (Ed.,) personality and Behaviour Disorder. 1 New York: Ronald press, 1944.

31. **Sanmugaganesan V.** "Effects of anxiety on Adjustment and achievement of professional students", unpublished Ph.D., Thesis, Annamalai University. (1996).

32. **Shah and Guha** "A study of adjustment and insecurity feeling among adolescents of two types of families". Journal of Education and psychology. 1985.

33. **Shah and Guha "**A study of adjustment and insecurity feeling among adolescents of two types of families". Journal of Education and psychology.

34. **Sharma, G.** "A study of factors underlying adjustment problem of professional and non-professional college students" Ph.D., in Education Meerut University R 1978.

35. **Sherman, M., and Joast,** "Frustration reactions of normal and neurotic persons", Journal of Psychology, Vol. 133, 3-19. 1942.

36. **Sinha A.**P. **and R.P. Singh Mannel** of adjustment Inventory for school students (AISS), National Psychological corporation 1984.

37. **Smith K.**V. **and Smith W.H.** The behaviours of man' Introduction to Psychology, Holt Rinehart and Winston Inc. 1958.

38. **Steinzor, B.** "Rorschach responses of achieving and non achieving students of high ability" American Journal of Psychometric 14. PP 494-504. 1944.

39. **Steven Richfield** "Social maturity strategy sheet" WWW Google, Com 2004.

40. **Stromcold, S.A and Wrem C.G.** "Counseling students towards school and adjustment". Educational and Psychological Measurement, 8 pp 57-63 (1948)

41. **Vinitha,** "A study of relationship between academic anxiety and adjustment among high school students". Indian Journal of behaviour Vol 7(1) 16-21 (1993)

42. **Young C.N.** "Scholarship and Social Adjustment" School and Society 43, 607-688. 1936

43. **Young K.,** Drought, "Social and Emotional adjustment of freshmen in the Universtiy of Wisconsin" Journal of Abnormal Sociology 2, 166-167 1937

APPENDIX

Dear Students,

Please fill up the following information's. It will be used for my research purpose.

Name	:	
Sex	:	Male / Female
Place of residence	:	Rural / Urban
Education	:	literate / illiterate
Type of Management	:	Govt. / Private

SOCIAL MATURITY SCALE

We face and experience several situations in our daily life. In everyone of these situations, we have a view of our own. Some such situations, where each one may have an opinion, are given below in the form of statements. Read them carefully. Each statement has a range of four responses. They are: **Strongly Agree (SA), Agree (A), Disagree (D), Strongly Disagree (DS),** Each response denotes are different position. Out of which, you should choose any one response which suggest your stand in respect of the statement, Accordingly, put a tick mark in the appropriate column.

S. No.	Statements	Strongly Agree (S.A)	Agree (A)	Disagree (D)	Strongly Disagree (DS)
1.	It is hard to stick to anything that takes a long time to do.				
2.	I often forget to listen to what others are saying				
3.	I would never go out of my way to help another person if it means giving up some personal pleasure.				
4.	The future is so uncertain, one cannot really make any plan.				
5.	There is no way to tell whom you can trust.				
6.	I cannot be friendly with people who do things which I consider wrong.				
7.	I get extremely hurt when people criticize me.				
8.	I fight to the last with my group if they do not carry out what I tell them.				
9.	Women should not be elected to top government positions.				
10.	I often forget work I am supposed to do.				
11.	I find it hard to speak my though clearly.				
12.	I am willing to give a lot of money to medical research on cancer or such deadly disease only if I know they would find a cure in my life time.				
13.	I feel very uncomfortable when I disagree with what my friends think.				
14.	Most people, I feel, would rather lie than speak the truth if they could get away with it.				
15.	I do not make close friends with crippled / handicapped persons though I do not like to admit this.				

S. No.	Statements	Strongly Agree (S.A)	Agree (A)	Disagree (D)	Strongly Disagree (DS)
16.	It is natural for anybody to feel extremely uneasy to speak to people whom he . she does not known.				
17.	I settle fights and differences among my friends.				
18.	A man should not cook dinner for his wife and children unless the wife is sick.				
19.	I often get behind in my work.				
20.	In a discussion, it is hard to understand what people are trying to say				
21.	I often think about has to tell me what to do				
22.	Someone often has to tell me what to do.				
23.	There are more bad people than good people in this world.				
24.	There are a lot of useful things for us to learn from having a group of people of other communities living in our neighborhood.				
25.	One feels miserable when one has to disagree with his friends.				
26.	I get along well with teachers and classmates in my school.				
27.	Many more women should be trained for jobs, usually held by men.				
28.	I often don't finish the work I start				
29.	Even if I know how to do something, I find it hard to teach someone else				
30.	Members of one religion should never ask money for some religious cause from				

S. No.	Statements	Strongly Agree (S.A)	Agree (A)	Disagree (D)	Strongly Disagree (DS)
31.	Others seem more in control of their lives than I do				
32.	It is hard to ask even the best friend for help.				
33.	One should not offer food to people who belong to other caste as it is embarrassing to refuse food offered.				
34.	I am comfortable only with people of my own sex				
35.	It is obvious that one gets upset when one has to change all his / her plans adjust to someone else.				
36.	If we do not encourage women to work, we are seriously reducing what the country could accomplish				
37.	I trend to go from one thing to another before finishing the earlier one.				
38.	It is hard for me to find anything to talk about when I meet a new person.				
39.	I want to spend more time in work to help the society I live in.				
40.	I keep my ideas to myself, in class unless I am sure I am right				
41.	You can be sure that people will be honest with you if you are honest with them.				
42.	I would not mind living next door to a family that is much poorer than mine.				
43.	It is a source of great disappointment to me when the opinion of other differs from mine.				
44.	There is no point helping, others inconveniencing oneself				

S. No.	Statements	Strongly Agree (S.A)	Agree (A)	Disagree (D)	Strongly Disagree (DS)
45.	I really worry the way many girls become doctors, engineers and lawyers these days.				
46.	I get upset if I am not immediately successful in learning something new.				
47.	My friends find it hard to figure out from what I say				
48.	Why work for something that others will enjoy when you won't be able to enjoy yourself.				
49.	In a group, I prefer to let other people make the decision				
50.	Even though it is hard to believe, the radio and newspaper give us true facts about important events.				
51.	I do not mind playing with people who speak a language different from mine.				
52.	One should be able to laugh at oneself and take jokes easily.				
53.	If you haven't been chosen as the leader, you should not suggest how things, should be done.				
54.	More men should train themselves for jobs like nursery school teachers and telephone operators which are usually held by women.				
55.	I often don't get my most important work done because I have spent too much time on another work.				
56.	In a discussion, people find it easy to understand what I am trying to say.				
57.	I would be willing to work for a good plan to make a better life for the poor, even if it costs me money.				

S. No.	Statements	Strongly Agree (S.A)	Agree (A)	Disagree (D)	Strongly Disagree (DS)
58.	I usually let others take the lead.				
59.	If you can trust a person in one way, you know you can trust him in all the ways.				
60.	I find more interest to work for friends whose caste is the same as mine.				
61.	It is obvious that one gets angry when one loses an argument.				
62.	In my class, I need not accept any responsibility in which I am not interested.				
63.	If everyone is to really equal, some people will have fewer advantages than they have now.				
64.	I give up the work I am doing, when things go wrong.				
65.	I am not good at describing things in writing.				
66.	It is possible to rush to neighbours to help them in all their troubles and needs.				
67.	The outcome of my life is a matter of luck.				
68.	A person is better off if he does not trust anybody.				
69.	I do not care to tell my ideas about god, when I know others will disagree with me.				
70.	I cannot keep cool when I get upset even though I am in a class room or in a formal group.				
71.					
72.	Giving higher education to woman is a national waste				
73.	Hard work is never a fund				
74.	I have a talent for influencing people by just talking to them.				

S. No.	Statements	Strongly Agree (S.A)	Agree (A)	Disagree (D)	Strongly Disagree (DS)
75.	A persons should not be excepted to do anything for his community unless he is paid for it.				
76.	When things have gone wrong for me, it is usually because of something I could not do anything about it.				
77.	A person who is completely trusting will have better experience in life than someone who is not.				
78.	I prefer to break with a friend who disagrees with me often.				
79.	I will not do the work I do not like though I am excepted to do				
80.	I make my point clear when I argue				
81.	I do not care to cut the use of water and electricity with a view to helping the government when there are so many others who are wasting it.				
82.	I do not know, whether, I like a new dress clothes / sari . until I find out what my friends think.				
83.	One can safety trust strangers as much as people they know.				
84.	It is very difficult for me to be nice to people I do not like.				
85.	It is more important for a job to pay well than to be interesting.				
86.	I understand what the teacher wants me to do.				
87.	I clean the papers off my desk around the place even though I did not put them.				

S. No.	Statements	Strongly Agree (S.A)	Agree (A)	Disagree (D)	Strongly Disagree (DS)
88.	It is not really all that important to do the home-work regularly.				
89.	I would find hard to give a talk in front of other in my class.				
90.	I would not mind giving money to a benefit fund for a school or hospital building even though it is not built in my own place.				

ADJUSTMENT

If answer is 'Yes' put a tick (✓)mark in the Yes, if the answer is no put a tick (✓)mark is 'No'

S. No.	Statement	Yes	No
1.	Are you always afraid of something in your school?		
2.	Do you avoid meeting you classmates?		
3.	Do you forget soon what you have read?		
4.	Suppose, your classmates, something unreasonable, unknowingly, do you immediately get angry with them?		
5.	Are you of a shy nature?		
6.	Are you afraid of examination?		
7.	Do you worried of your teacher scolding you for your mistakes		
8.	Do you hesitate in asking a question when you don't understand something?		
9.	Is it difficult for you to understand the lessons taught in the class?		
10.	Are you jealous of those friends whom teachers appreciate much?		
11.	When some of your teachers are together, do you go there without any complex?		
12.	Can you note down the lessons taught in the class correctly?		
13.	Do you envy those classmates whom you thing are better than you?		

14. Do you feel sometimes, as if you have no friends in your school?
15. Do you yawn when lesson is taught in your class?
16. When you see, some students talking themselves, do you think they are gossiping about you?
17. Are you able to get friendly easily?
18. Are you satisfied with the method of the teaching of the teachers of this school.
19. Do you express your anger to others when you are not asked to come forward in any program in your school?
20. When some students are talking together, do you join them freely?
21. Do you think that the teachers in the school do not give any attention to your problem?
22. Are you often sad and distressed in the school?
23. Do you like to join your classmates in the school?
24. Are you satisfied with progress sin you studies?
25. Do you feel that the teachers neglect you?
26. Do you try to attract the attention of your teacher to yourself in the class?
27. Is it a burden for you to study?
28. Do you get yourself worked up and try to harm a student when he complains against you?
29. Do you often like to be alone?
30. Are your teacher always ready to solve your problems concerning your studies?
31. Are you often dissatisfied with your school?
32. Do you establish a friendly relationship with the students in the school?
33. Do you teachers in the school praise you?
34. Do you try to rationalize you mistake?
35. Do you like to sit in the front seats in the class?
36. Do you often get less marks in examinations?
37. Do you resent it when your teachers ask you a question in the class?
38. Do you have a friendly association with your fellow student?
39. Do you like the idea of having more holidays in the school?
40. Do you get wild when one of your classmates jokes with you?

41. Do you openly take part in the school assemblies?
42. Do you often quarrel with your classmates?
43. Do you sometimes go home before the school closes?
44. Do you take part in the school sports?
45. Do some of your teachers often keep on scolding you for the studies?
46. Do you often have doubt on others in the school?
47. Are you shy of talking to the senior students in the school?
48. Do you look at your teachers respectively?
49. Do you show impertinence (arrogance) towards something good sent by a mate with whom you don't get along well.
50. Do you have some intimate friends in this school?
51. Do you pay attention of the lesson being taught in the class?
52. Do you develop resentful feelings towards your teachers when you get less unlike?
53. Are you always ready to help your classmates in every way?
54. Do you borrow the books and magazines from the school library and read them?
55. Are you often afraid of meetings the senior students?
56. Do you enjoy irritating other students in the school?
57. Do you take part in the debates?
58. Do you feel mentally depressed when you meet the senior students?
59. Do you lend your books or not books gladly when your class-mates ask for it?
60. Are you interested in the things regarding education?

2. Social Intelligence and Social Maturity

Problem and its perspectives

Emergence of the study

Every difference of environment means a difference in one's habit and one's way of living in so far as these differences create a different environment, a dynamic equilibrium of life is maintained through a processing of constant selections and constant adaptations. The society is not the world but is directly related to every one's life and maturity. The more complex the adaptation with society becomes, the more complex the social maturity and intelligence. Society and environment is essential for development of intelligence, maturity according to the need.

Society is a significant medium where certain quality of life and certain types of activity and occupation are provided with the aim of securing child's development based on the social needs. Since it is a stem of growth characteristics of an adolescent period by which every student should adapt to the society in which we live and to which he is expected to adjust and contribute, the social intelligence and maturity receives importance at the present context. The conduct of many individual in the society tells about his intelligence and social maturity through which he can respond right according to situations.

At the present age of competitive world, every human being meets a lot of problems in his daily activities. The root of most of human psychological problems are more socially based than psychologically based. Their problems are not mental illness. It is social incompetence, a lack of social intelligence as well as social maturity. So every human need knowledge about social intelligence and social maturity for leading a very healthy life in this world.

The present study takes a position that social intelligence and maturity are very important to the students who live and grow in the complex social environment. Hence there is a need to find out if there is any correlation between social intelligence and social maturity. Hence the problem emerged to study the two variables social intelligence and social maturity.

Statement of the problem

The title of the problem is as follows: *A Study of Social Intelligence and Social Maturity among Arts and Science College students.*

Operational Definitions

Social Intelligence

Social intelligence means ability of an individual to react to social situations of daily life. Social intelligence would not include the feelings or emotions aroused in us by other people, but merely our ability to understand others and to react in such a way towards them that the ends desired should be attained. High social intelligence is possessed by those who are able to handle people well. Adequate adjustment in social situations is the index of social intelligence.

VERNON (1933) defined social intelligence as the "Person's ability to get along with people in general, social technique or case in society, knowledge of social matters, susceptibility to stimuli from other members of a group, as well as insight into the temporary moods and underlying personality traits of strangers".

E.L.THORNDIKE (1920) has pointed out that there is an aspect of personality that can be called "Social Intelligence", distinct from, "Concrete" and "Abstract" intelligence,

STERNBERY (1984), defines Intelligence as "Consisting of purposive selection and shaping of an adaptation to real-world environments relevant to one's life".

Social Maturity

Maturity assumes accountability, constantly assesses, judges and takes appropriate decisions. Maturity develops a balanced emotional outlook, helping the individual to accept himself, his talents and limitations and to accept others as they are. It analysis values and internalizes them consistently. It helps towards progressive advancement in spiritual growth, impelling the individual to adapt himself to change and to life without emotional crisis.

ABRAHAM SPERLING (1967) defined social maturity in the following words, "An adolescent should get along with others. He ought to develop self-reliance in matters of taste and ought to develop tolerance of human differences".

NAZARATH MARIA E. WAPLES (1978) defines as, "Maturity is the blossoming of man's character into a unified totality. It discerns the process that contribute to the psychological and physical growth and well being of man".

HENRY E GARRETT (1968) states, "Social maturity is the degree of social participation as measured by child's activities, attitudes and play interests. It is related to physical growth and maturity and to mental ability. Every individual develops his own unique way of adjustment in the society. An individual, since his birth attempts to adjust to his environment".

Importance of Social Intelligence

Social intelligence is at the heart of human happiness and emotional comfort.

Explored further, the reason for unhappiness is the inability to maintain positive human relationships with the society. The result will be depression, fear, confusion and anger, created by the lack of positive human emotions that are critical to the happiness of us all. So social intelligence is very important in human's life that is created to bring the practical technology of skills-based training into the world of human interaction and relations.

Need for Social Intelligence

Although anyone can benefit from social intelligence training, it has been especially successful with the following group.

1. People in high stress jobs.
2. Single or divorced men and women who would like to find and build a healthy relationship.
3. Senior - mid level managers.
4. Workers in a regular contact with public.

Factors of Social Intelligence

The following factors are mostly including in the concept of social intelligence.

Patience, Co-cooperativeness, Confidence level, Sensitivity, Recognitions of social environment, Tactfulness, Sense of humours and memory.

? **Patience**: Calm endurable under stressful situation.

? **Co-cooperativeness**: Ability to interact with others in a pleasant way to be able to view matters from all angles.

? **Confidence Level**: Form trust in one self and one's chances.

? **Sensitivity**: To be acutely aware of and being responsive.

? **Recognition of social environment**: Ability to perceive the nature and atmosphere of the existing situation.

? **Tactfulness**: Delicate perception of the right thing to say or do.

? **Sense of humours**: Capacity to feel and cause amusement; to be able to see the lighter side of life.

? **Memory**: Ability to remember all relevant issues; names and faces of people.

Stages of Social Maturity

An individual takes times in his social development. So, we may think of some stages of social maturity according to the physical, mental, emotional and language development of the individual. They are,

? Awareness of the presence of another person.

? Mixing with others.

? Understanding of social relationships.

Understanding of all the above three things refers to human stages of social maturity.

Social Maturity and its characteristics

Social maturity is the final expected outcome of social development and socialization, certain characteristics of social maturity are, a) A socially matured person has a sense of his proper place and role as a member of the social group. He is willing and able to orient himself in the various activities and customs to the group.

(b) He is able to assume a reasonable amount of responsibility, to adjust him to the inevitable limitations and restrictions of the community life.

(c) He can be original and yet conform to the broad pattern of his social environment. d) He evaluates social problems not from a purely selfish point of view but has regard to the right opinion of others.

(e) He accepts responsibility for his actions, does not indulge in self-pitying.

(f) He has a realistic self-concept being conscious of his assets and limitations.

(g) He is relatively secure and so open to new experiences, which contribute, to his continuous development.

In short, co-operation, pleasing manner, consideration for others, positive and optimistic outlook on life and social intelligence are signs of socially matured individual.

Importance of Social Maturity

Social maturity has been defined as an indication of willingness and ability to orient oneself in the various activities and customs of the group to make a proportionate contribution to the work to be done, to take a suitable part in the social exchange, to assume a reasonable amount of responsibility and to adjust oneself to the inevitable limitations and restrictions of community life without waste of energy or loss of satisfaction.

Significance of the study

A new concept social intelligence with its significance is more important for one's daily life. It may be defined as one's unitary ability to know, feel, judge, behave and cooperate with a person's thinking process for behaving in a proper way with the ultimate realization of happiness in him and in others. In view of its wide significance from the individual as well as social angles, it becomes quite imperative that serious efforts should be made for its proper development right from early child hood among human beings.

A person's social intelligence helps him much in all spheres of life. Social intelligence also helps a person to understand and give direction to live a very healthy life.

Social intelligence and social maturity are important for survival, decision making, boundary setting, communication and making unity in society, which are very essential to makes ones life's happy.

Every human being should have the knowledge of good social relationship. The social intelligence makes ones knowledge good in social relationship. Therefore social intelligence and social maturity plays very essential and significant role in humans, who are want to live a happy social life.

Objectives of the study

The following are the objectives of the present study:

1. To find out the level of social intelligence of Arts and Science college students.

2. To find out the level of social maturity of Arts and Science college students.
3. To find out the relationship between social intelligence and social maturity among Arts and Science college students.
4. To find out the significant difference between boys and girls on their social intelligence among Arts and Science colleges.
5. To find out the significant difference between boys and girls on their social maturity among Arts and Science colleges.
6. To find out the significant difference between rural and urban environment on their social intelligence among Arts and Science colleges.
7. To find out the significant difference between rural and urban environment on their social maturity among Arts and Science colleges.
8. To find out the significant difference of social intelligence of Arts and Science college students based on their college type.
9. To find out the significant difference of social maturity of Arts and Science college students based on their college type.
10. To find out the significant difference between government and government aided college students on their social intelligence among Arts and Science Colleges.
11. To find out the significant difference between government and government aided college students on their social maturity among Arts and Science Colleges.
12. To find out the significant difference between nuclear and joint family students on their social intelligence among Arts and Science college students.
13. To find out the significant difference between nuclear and joint family students on their social maturity among Arts and Science college students.
14. To find out the significant difference of social intelligence of Arts and Science college students based on their parental income.

15. To find out the significant difference of social maturity of Arts and Science college students based on their parental income.

Limitations

The present investigation has the following limitations.

1. The investigation is limited to Arts and Science college students.
2. The study is restricted to three colleges.
3. The sample is restricted to 300 students.

Conclusion

The problem of the present study has been discussed briefly in this chapter, bringing out the characteristics, importance and objectives of the study etc. A detailed discussion of the related literature follows in the next chapter.

Review of related literature

Introduction

The researcher takes the advantage of the knowledge, which has accumulated in the past as a result of constant human endeavour. Research can never be undertaken in isolation of the work that has already been done on the problem, which is directly or indirectly related to study proposed by a researcher. One of the important steps in the planning of any research study is careful review of the research journals, books, dissertations, and other series of information on the problem to be investigated. A review of the related literature must precede any well-planned research study.

Review of the related literature allows the researcher to acquaint him with current knowledge in the field or area in which he is going to conduct his research. The important specific reason for reviewing the related literature is to know about the recommendation of previous researchers for further research, which they have listed in their studies. The present summary of research studies are related to the problem "Social Intelligence and Social Maturity" among Arts and Science college students.

Studies Related to Social Intelligence

Indian Studies

The study was undertaken by **Buch.M.B** (1960) for assessing the social intelligence of individuals quantitatively and to study the effect of environmental factors as grade as occupational status of social intelligence. The subjects for the present study of social intelligence were selected on the basis of certain independent findings supported by the content analysis of the available tests of social intelligence. The sub tests included were (1) judgment in social situations. (2) Memory for names and faces. (3) Observation of human behaviors. (4) Recognition of the mental state. (5) Sense of humor. (6) Social Introduction. The major findings indicated that the environmental factors very much influenced the social intelligence of individuals.

Ray. T (1972) aimed at developing test in Bengali for the objective measurement of social intelligence. The final form of the test had eighty items distributed on six subjects corresponding to six different areas of human behaviour namely (1) judgment in social situations. (2) Observation of human behaviors. (3) Recognition of the mental state. (4) Memory for names and faces. (5) Appreciation of humour. (6) Adjustment. The findings revealed that the human behaviour had very significant relationship to social intelligence.

On examining the social interest and attitude of college students and to see how these attitudes will influence their future family organization. **Singhai. S** (1986) found that the social interests and attitude of adolescent students were adequate, mature and stable. It was found that suitable environment influenced development of healthy social interest and attitude of student.

R. Lenin (2005) conducted an investigation into emotional intelligence and social intelligence of teacher trainees, who were studying under University of Madras. The shamble consists of 293 students from six teacher-training colleges in Chennai. It was found that the level of social intelligence and emotional intelligence of teacher trainees is moderate in nature and there is a significant relation between emotional intelligence and social intelligence.

Vootnoori Rajesh (2006) conducted the study, which was analysing the achievement in social science with related to emotional maturity and social intelligence of 308 secondary school students in karimnagar District, Andra Pradesh . It was found that the level of emotional maturity and social intelligence of secondary school students and level of achievement in social science of secondary school students is moderate in nature. It was found that there is significant association between emotional maturity and social intelligence.

Foreign Studies

A study was done by **Brar S** (1992) to examine the social emotional competence of pre-school children and relationship to intelligence and maturity. A study verifies empirically whether social emotional competence depends on the intelligence and social maturity of young children who were under taken in India. A standardized intelligence test was administered to the children to assess social emotional competence and social maturity. Based on test and observation results, children were categorized into groups of high and low intelligence and into groups of high and low social maturity. Scores for the group were compared with respect to four aspects of social emotional competence: (1) Self-confident (2) Antonomy-dependance (3) Quality of social interaction and (4) coping technique.

A study was done by **Gabriellsen, Eric** (1992) to examine the role of self-monitoring in the choice of college major. A self monitoring person is an individual who adopts a social orientation so that he can manage self presenting, self monitors are likely to modify their academic choices to fit social situations or others expectations. Data were collected using a four-part questionnaire that explored background, a self-monitoring scale, a personal freedom versus social conformity scale and a friendship scale. Result indicated that self-monitors played a role in selection of college majors. However, data and findings also indicated that the direct influence of close friends was not what most presented self-monitors with regard to choice of major.

Chen-shyuefee, Agens; Michael, William B. (1993) has investigated first order and higher order factors of creative social intelligence with in Guilford's structure -of - intellect model . The study carried out how accurately each of several hypothesized combinations of first- order and higher - order factors reflecting creativity in the social intelligence of 192 high school students described the covariation in selected submatrixes from the total correlation matrix originally analyzed. Results support Guilford,s structure of intellect model.

Studies related to Social Maturity

Indian Studies

Ghosh. S (1975) has investigated social maturity of preschool Bengali children of Calcutta city belonging to different social-economic groups. Thirty five, nursery and kinder garden schools were randomly selected from the different regions of Calcutta and 40 pre-school children were selected from each school at random equally distributed in each age group. Data were also collected by using a standardized interview schedule on the mothers of these selected children. The final sample included 1410 cases. The study revealed that sex had very insignificant role in imbibing social maturation. Economic status was insignificant as testimony of ability to enrich the social maturity level.

Rao.N. (1978) conducted a research work on social maturity of high school children in Bangalore city. A sample of 1020 students were chosen from 50 secondary schools in Bangalore. The self-constructed questionnaire was used in this study. The major findings were as follows; (I) positive correlation between social maturity and intelligence (II) positive relationship between social maturities and self-esteem. (III) Girls generally scored higher than boys on social maturity. (IV) There were class differences in social maturity among the children of lower grades. (V) Private school children scored more on social maturity than government schools.

Puranik, S.D (1985) has studied the relationship of social maturity of pupils with organizational climate and teacher's morale in the primary schools of Banglore city. The sample consists of 70 schools 2634 students and 712 teachers. The study indicated the development of social maturity; autonomous climate, private management and unaided students and urban location of schools were most conductive factors. No effect of moral of teachers of both senses was noticed on the development of social maturity of male (or) female students (or) on the students of both sexes even under the influence of organizational climate, school organization and localities.

Asthana, Anju (1989) conducted a study of social maturity among school going children in city of Lucknow. The Objectives were, (I) To study whether social maturity increases with grade level. (II) To study association of intelligence, socio-economic status academic achievement, adult dependence and sex of the child with social maturity. It was found that the Social maturity increased with inverse in grade level, the growth rate being highest in the first school years. Intelligence, academic achievement and adult dependence were significantly associated with the social maturity of children although adult dependence and a negative association and SES was not found to contribute to social maturity at any of the five grade levels.

Sarojamma, Y.H. (1990) has conducted a comparative study of reading ability and social maturity of over normal and underachievers of standard VIII, the final sample comprised of 476 boys and 524 girls. The social maturity scale by Sathyanarayana and Swadha was used. It was found that, there was significant difference in the reading ability of,

(a) Normal and under achievers,
(b) Over and normal achievers,
(c) Girls and boys,
(d) Students having high and low social maturity (f) Students in private and government schools.

The interaction effect of the variables on reading ability, hypothesized were not significant.

Malin, A.J. (1990) conducted a study on the relationship of social maturity with classroom climate and academic achievement. The sample consisted of 1200 students of classes VIII and IX. The tools used were Edwards's social maturity state and achievements test. The research points out students studying in classes IX had higher maturity as compared to students of class VIII. The mean maturity scores of students having low achievement for both classes. Classroom climate and achievement has a significant effort on maturity scores of students of both the class.

Agnihotri, C.S. (1991) has conducted a cross cultural comparative study between tribal and non tribal first generation and traditional learners in relation to their social maturity and educational adjustment. The sample consisted of 113 first generation tribal learners and 108 traditional tribal learners. Social maturity was independent of traditions of learning. The tribal and non-tribal differed in terms of their placements on attribute of social maturity. The traditions of learning were found to be contributing to social maturity. It was found that, the social maturity and educational adjustment were only social ingredients. Psychological characteristics also influenced the social maturity and educational adjustment of children and social maturity was independent of traditions of learning.

Bhushan, A. (1994) conducted a study on social maturity across sex and family vocations. The sample comprised of 200 student teachers from two colleges, equally divided between two sexes. Major variable used were sex values, and family vocations. The tools used for data collections were the form D of value survey. The study highlights, male and female uniformly assigned highest importance to social maturity. Both male and female from service and non-service class had politeness as a subdivision on their maturity.

Foreign Studies

Vora, J.I (1980) in his research work on social maturity of B.Ed., students in Gujarat. The sample size was 855 student teachers from Gujarat University, South Gujarat University and M.S. University. Some of the major findings were (I) The male students were superior to the female students in their social maturity (II) Age had no relation with social maturity (III) The arts students were more socially mature than science students. (IV) The higher socio-economic status had better social maturity.

Saovoluk Thongngamkhom (1983) has investigated the social maturity as a function of some psycho socio- adjustment factors of B.Ed college students of north central region of Thailand. The scale was standardized on a sample of 922 students-including boys and girls. The study states that boys and girls having dominant personality traits were more socially matured than those having submissive personality traits. The two groups of B.Ed., students having high suggestibility and low suggestibility trait did not differ on social maturity. The study revealed that the college students with high SES background were found more socially matured than those of coming from low SES strata. The students having dominant personality trait were more socially matured than those of having submissive personality trait. The students having high leadership personality trait were more socially matured than those of having low leadership personality trait.

Pattramon JumpanGern (1986) investigated the social maturity of teachers, college students of western region of Thailand and found that the teachers - college student coming from urban areas were found to be more matured than those coming from rural areas. Students having good family adjustment were more socially matured than those having poor family adjustment. It was found that the higher secondary students coming from urban areas were found to be more matured than those coming from rural areas. The male higher secondary students were found superior to the female students. The higher secondary students with high SES were more socially matured than those with low SES.

Bancs Ann Leslie (1995) conducted a study on measuring the effect of participation in a peer facilitation project on sixth graders self esteem, social maturity and patterns of social choice. The population chosen for the study was rural mainstream sixth grade students. The sample was tested by sociometric pattern of choice. It was found that some significant difference in social maturity for gender and there was significant relationship between self-esteem and social maturity.

Mulia, R.D (1991). A comparative study of the social maturity of higher secondary students in the contest of their streams, sex and IQs. The objectives were, (I) To study the stream effect on social maturity. (II) To study the sex effect on social maturity. (III) To study the effect of levels of IQs on social maturity. (IV) To study the interaction effect among independent variables on social maturity. It was found that there was no significant relationship in social maturity among students of three streams and between the two sexes, while IQ had main significant effect on social maturity streams and sex and no interaction effect of streams and sex as well as sex and IQs was found significant on social maturity.

Flymin Xavier, J., (2003) attempted a study on social maturity and academic achievement among higher secondary school students. The sample of 300 were taken from government, government aided and private higher secondary schools in Trivandram. The sample were tested by Rao's Social maturity scale. Some of the major findings were (i) Gender has no influence on social maturity (ii) Type of schools had no influence on social maturity (iii) Social maturity and academic achievement are positively correlated.

Mani, M., (2004) did his study on social maturity and adherence to school regulation of higher secondary students. Taken the sample of 300 higher secondary school students studying in 5diffrent schools in Chennai. Rao's social maturity scale was used for administration. Some of the major findings were (I) Gender has significant bearing on social maturity (II) There is significant relationship between social maturity and adherence to school regulations (III) There is significant relationship between social maturity and academic achievement.

Saravanan, K., (2005) attempted a research on social maturity on self-concept among higher secondary school students. The sample of 249 boys and girls who studied XI standard in various schools in Chennai was taken. Rao's social maturity scale was used for administration. Some of the major findings were (I) Social maturity is found to be moderate. (II) Gender has no influence on social maturity. (III) Type of school had no significant difference on social maturity.

Conclusion

The survey of related literature has helped the investigator to have clear perspective of the problem chosen for the above review of related literature that very few studies had been carried out using both variables “social intelligence” and “social maturity”. Hence the investigator has chosen to study these two variables on college students. The reviews based on Indian and foreign studies, had helped the researcher to frame appropriate hypotheses. light of the literature studied, the third chapter has been designed.

Research Design and Methods of Investigation

Introduction

This chapter gives an overall picture of the design of the study, research tools used for the study, nature and selection of the sample and a brief description of the procedure adopted for the collection of data, in the light of other research studies.

Thyer (1993) defined research design as "a blue print for how research study is to be completed operationalising variables so they can be measured, selecting a sample of interest to study collecting data to be used as a basis for testing hypothesis and analyzing the results".

Research is always directed towards solution to a problem. It is a procedure from known to unknown. The ultimate goal of any research work is to find out the cause and effect relationship between the variables.

Hypotheses

The following hypotheses are set for the present study.

1. The level of social intelligence of Arts and Science college students is moderate in nature.
2. The level of social maturity of Arts and Science college students is moderate in nature.

3. There is a significant relationship between social intelligence and social maturity among Arts and Science college students.
4. There is a significant difference between boys and girls on their social intelligence among Arts and Science College.
5. There is a significant difference between boys and girls on their social maturity among Arts and Science College.
6. There is a significant difference between rural and urban environment on their social intelligence among Arts and Science college students.
7. There is a significant difference between rural and urban environment on their social maturity among Arts and Science college students.
8. There is no significant difference of social intelligence of Arts and Science college students based on their college type.
9. There is no significant difference of social maturity of Arts and Science college students based on their college type.
10. There is no significant difference between government and government aided college students on their social intelligence among Arts and Science college students.
11. There is no significant difference between government and government aided on their social maturity among Arts and Science college students.
12. There is a significant difference between nuclear and joint family students on their social intelligence among Arts and Science college students.
13. There is a significant difference between nuclear and joint family students on their social maturity among Arts and Science college students.
14. There is a significant difference in social intelligence of Arts and Science college students based on their parental income.
15. There is a significant difference in social maturity of Arts and Science college students based on their parental income.

Description of the tools used

To verify the framed hypotheses the following tools and techniques were used in the present investigation.

1. Social Intelligence scale.
2. Social Maturity scale.

Social Intelligence scale

Description of the tool

This test consists of 54 items and photographs of 12 eminent persons constructed by Dr.N.K.Chadha. This tool deals with 8 factors of social intelligence. They are patience, confidence, cooperativeness, sensitivity, tactfulness, sense of humours, memory, and recognition of social environment.

Administration

The investigator established rapport with the students and explained the purpose of the investigation. The investigator made the arrangements for investigation and informed to the students that they were not being tested, and their responses would be kept confidential in the strict sense. Then the inventory was distributed to the class and the students were asked to record their responses by putting a (X) mark against every statement on the answer sheet. In part V, the list of eminent persons were given. The students were asked to write their names on the answer sheet.

Scoring

In the case of the first four dimensions patience, cooperativeness, confidence, and sensitivity, scores of 1, 2, and 3 were given to three response alternatives. For e.g., in the confidence dimension a score of 3 would indicate a high degree of confidence, a score of 1 a lack of confidence and a score of 2 would reveal moderate confidence. In the other two dimensions (sense of humour and Recognition of social environment) one of three alternatives given is the appropriate response. This response when given was allotted to scores of 1. In the case of the "Tactfulness" dimension the response was awarded a score of "1" the last dimension that of memory was scored "1" or "0" depending on whether or not the subjects response was "right" or "wrong".

Social Maturity scale

Description of the tool

The maturity outcomes of school going population can best be estimated in the light of paucity of such essential increasing instruments. The social maturity scale was developed by "Dr. Nalini Rao", Department of Education, Bangalore University. The framework for the integrated conceptual virtues of social maturity was adapted from the psychosocial structure.

It was formulated by Green Berger ET.AL. The final form of the questionnaire consists of 90 items know as "Rao's SOCIAL MATURITY SCALE" (RSMS).

Administration

The social maturity scales were administrated to the respondents in groups in the regular classroom situation. The instruction provided on the first page of the scale booklet is self-explanatory. Reading of the instructions by the examiner to the group however ensures better conditions for responding to the items of the scale. The answers were recorded by the respondent on the scale protocol.

The item required to complete the scale items are between 45 minutes and one hour classification sought by the student regarding any item is to be handled by the examiner through encouraging the respondents. In this way the administration procedure is carried out.

Scoring

The final form of the questionnaire consists of 90 items. Each item was accorded a four point response speed, the intervals of which are labeled.

- Strongly agree
- Agree

- Disagree
- Strongly disagree

The successive response intervals were subsequently scored as 4, 3, 2 and 1 with the high score represents mature response. There were no right or wrong answers. The answers were checked against the key and point is given for each item ticked as per the key. The total point obtained gives a measure of social maturity.

By this way the scoring is carried out for social maturity.

Table 1

Scoring key of the questionnaire according to the nature of items

Nature of Item	Strongly Agree	Agree	Strongly Disagree	Disagree
Positive 17, 21, 24, 26, 36, 39, 41, 42, 50, 51, 52, 54, 56, 57, 59, 63, 74, 77, 89, 90	4	3	2	1
Negative 1, 2, 3, 4, 5, 6, 7, 8, 9, 10, 11, 12, 13, 14, 15, 16, 18, 19, 20, 22, 23, 25, 27, 28, 29, 30, 31, 32, 33, 34, 35, 37, 38, 40, 43, 44, 45, 46, 47, 48, 49, 53, 55, 58, 61, 62, 63, 64, 65, 66, 67, 68, 69, 70, 71, 72, 73, 75, 76, 78, 79, 80, 81, 82, 83, 84, 85, 86, 87, 88	1	2	3	4

Pilot Study:

A pilot study was conducted on 50 students to establish the reliability and validity of the different tools used in the present study.

Establishing reliability and validity

The reliability of a test may be defined as the degree of consistency with which the test measures what it does measure. A test score is called reliable to be stable and trustworthy. The reliability of the tool was calculated using Spearman Brown's formula for split half method.

$$r_{11} = \frac{2r_{hh}}{1 + r_{hh}}$$

r_{11} = Reliability coefficient of the whole test.

r_{hh} = Reliability coefficient of the half-test, found experimentally. .

Social Intelligence scale

Reliability

In order to establish the reliability of the social intelligence scale, the split half method was used. The reliability of social intelligence was found to be 0.817. Hence the social intelligence scale is considered as a reliable.

Validity

The index of validity, which is the square root of reliability, was found to be 0.9. Hence social intelligence scale selected for the study was considered to have high validity.

Social Maturity scale

Reliability

In order to establish the reliability of the social maturity scale, the split half method was used. The reliability of social maturity scale was found to be 0.76. Hence social intelligence scale is considered as a reliable tool.

Validity

The index of validity, which is the square root of reliability, was found to be 0.78. Hence social intelligence scale selection for the study was considered to have high valid.

Main Study

The validated scales were used to collect the necessary data for the main study. The study was carried out on a sample of 300 arts and science college students in the month of November 2006.

The sample was stratified on the basis of type of management viz, Government and Aided colleges and type of location viz, rural and urban environment.

It was also stratified on the basis of the type of college viz, Boys only, girls only and co education.

Table 2

The table shows the background variables of the samples.

College name	Type of College	College location	Type of management	No of samples
APA arts and science college for boys	Boys only	Urban	Government	90
APA arts and science college for girls	Girls only	Rural	Government	95
St Joseph's College.	Co education	Urban	Government Aided	115

Statistical Techniques used

Suitable descriptive and inferential statistical techniques were used in the interpretation of data to draw out a meaningful picture of results from the collected data. In the present study the following statistical measures were used.

Mean

$$X = A + \frac{\sum fd}{\sum f} \text{ x I}$$

Where,

A = Assumed mean

F = Frequency

D = Deviation from the assumed mean

I = Class interval

Standard Deviation

$$SD = \sigma\sqrt{\frac{\sum fd}{N} - \left(\frac{\sum fd}{N}\right)^2}$$

Where,

F = Frequency

D = Deviation from arithmetic mean

I = Class internal

ó = Standard deviation

Quartile Deviation

Q_1 = $L1 + \left(\frac{N/_4 - CF1}{F1}\right) x1$

Q_2 = $L3 + \left(\frac{3N/_4 - CF3}{F3}\right) x1$

Q_3 = $\frac{Q_3 - Q_1}{2}$

QD = Quartile Deviation

Q_1 = First QD

Q_3 = Third QD

L_1, L_3 = Lower limit of medium class

N = Total Frequency

CF1CF2 = Cumulative frequency

F1, F2 = Frequency of the medium class

$$\frac{\text{n dard error of mean deviation}}{\frac{\sigma_1^2}{N_1} + \frac{\sigma_2^2}{N_2}}$$

Standard Error Deviation

SEMD =

$ó_1$ = SD of group I variable

$ó_2$ = SD of group II variable

N_1, N_2 = Total number of sample for group I, ii

Critical Ratio

To compare the significance of difference between mean, critical ratio was used. Critical ratio was calculated from the relation.

$$C.R. = \frac{M_1 - M_2}{\sqrt{\frac{\sigma 1^2}{N_1} + \frac{\sigma 2^2}{N_2}}}$$

Where,

M.M = Mean of group, I, II variable

ó$_1$, ó$_2$	=	Standard Deviation
N_1, N_2	=	Total number of class

Analysis of Variance

Correlation coefficient (r)

r =

F-Ratio

$$\text{F-ratio} = \frac{\text{Variance between group}}{\text{Variance within - group}}$$

$$\text{Correlation term } C = \frac{\sum x_1 + \sum x_2 + \sum x_3}{N}$$

$$\text{Tss} = X_2\text{-C}$$

$$\text{Bss} = \frac{(\sum x_1)}{N} + \frac{(\sum x_2)}{N} + \frac{(\sum x_3)}{N}$$

$$\text{Wss} = \text{Tss - Bss}$$

Where

Óx$_1$, Óx$_2$, Óx$_3$ are scores in different groups.

C	=	Correlation term
Tss	=	Total sum of squares
Bss	=	Between sum of squares
Wss	=	Within sum of squares

Conclusion

This chapter indicates the details regarding the design of the study, hypotheses, pilot study and statistical techniques used. A detailed discussion of analysis of study and interpretation of the study follows in the next chapter.

Analysis and Interpretation of the data

Introduction

Research consists of systematic observation and description of the characteristics of properties for the purpose of discovering relationship starts with the description of the measures of the variables and goes on the higher level of statistics analysis. To develop the research plan, processing and analysis of data is necessary .It covers all the technical matters related to research work. This chapter describes the analysis of data and testing of hypotheses that have been framed on the basis of objectives, using appropriate statistical techniques. The data collected was carefully edited, systematically classified, tabulated, analyzed, interpreted and rationally concluded.

Testing of hypotheses

Hypothesis - I :

The level of social intelligence of Arts and Science college students is moderate in nature.

Table 3

Showing the level of social intelligence of Arts and Science college students.

Factor	Description	Number of Students	Percentage
Social Intelligence	Low	75	25.00
	Average	143	47.67

	High	82	27.33
	Total	300	100.00

Interpretation

From the above table it is clear that the level of social intelligence among arts and science college students is average in nature, confirming the hypothesis.

Hypothesis - II

The level of social maturity of Arts and Science college students is moderate in nature.

Table 4

Showing the level of social maturity of Arts and Science College.

Factor	Description	Number of Students	Percentage
Social Maturity	Low	78	26.00
	Average	141	47.00
	High	81	27.00
	Total	300	100.00

Interpretation

From the above table it is clear that the social maturity among arts and science college students is average in nature, confirming the hypothesis.

Hypothesis-III

There is a significant relationship between social intelligence and social maturity among Arts and Science college students.

Table 5

Showing the relationship between social intelligence and social maturity.

Factor	Number of students	Correlation	Level of significance
Social Intelligence and Social Maturity	300	0.79	0.01

Interpretation

From the above table it is clear that there is a relationship between social intelligence and social maturity among arts and science college students. Hence, the empirical hypothesis is accepted.

Hypothesis-IV

There is a significant difference between boys and girls on their social intelligence among Arts and Science college students.

Table 6

Showing the difference between boys and girls on their social intelligence.

Factor	Gender	Number of students	Mean	SD	SEMD	CR	L.S
Social Intelligence	Male	150	95.86	15.74	1.29	1.28	N.S
	Female	150	98.01	13.40	1.1		

Interpretation

From the above table it is clear that, there is no significant difference between boys and girls on their social intelligence among Arts and Science college students. Hence, the empirical hypothesis is rejected.

Hypothesis-V

There is a significant difference between boys and girls on their social maturity among Arts and Science college students.

Table 7

Showing the difference between boys and girls on their social maturity.

Factor	Gender	Number of students	Mean	SD	SEMD	CR	L.S
Social Maturity	Male	150	236.74	20.65	1.69	2.51	0.05
	Female	150	242.41	18.41	1.50		

Interpretation

From the above table it is clear that, there is no significant difference between boys and girls on their social maturity among Arts and Science college students. Hence, the empirical hypothesis is accepted.

Hypothesis-VI

There is a significant difference between rural and urban environment on their social intelligence among Arts and Science college students.

Table 8

Showing the significant difference between rural and urban environment on their social intelligence.

Factor	Gender	Number of students	Mean	SD	SEMD	CR	L.S
Social Intelligence	Rural	95	97.0	13.04	1.33	0.05	N.S
	Urban	205	96.91	15.34	1.07		

Interpretation

From the above table it is clear that, there is no significant difference between rural and urban environment on their social intelligence among Arts and Science college students. Hence the empirical hypothesis is rejected.

Table 9

Showing the significant difference between rural and urban environment on their social maturity.

Factor	Gender	Number of students	Mean	SD	SEMD	CR	L.S
Social Maturity	Rural	95	240.16	19.1	1.96	0.35	N.S
	Urban	205	239.31	20.1	1.40		

Hypothesis-VII

There is a significant difference between rural and urban environment on their social maturity among Arts and Science college students.

Interpretation

From the above table it is clear that, there is no significant difference between rural and urban environment on their social maturity among Arts and Science college students. Hence the empirical hypothesis is rejected.

Hypothesis-VIII

There is no significant difference in social intelligence of Arts and Science college students based on their college type.

Table 10

Showing the difference of social intelligence based on college type.

Factor	Source	DF	Sum of squares	Mean squares	F ratio	L.S
Social Intelligence	Between groups	2	1009.15	504.58	2.3787	N.S
	Within groups	297	63000.64	212.12		
	Total	299	64009.80			

Interpretation

From the above table it is clear that, there is no significant difference of intelligence of Arts and Science college students. Hence the null hypothesis is accepted.

Hypothesis-IX

There is no significant difference in social maturity of Arts and Science college students based on their college type.

Table 11

Showing the difference of social maturity based on college type.

Factor	Source	DF	Sum of squares	Mean squares	F ratio	L.S
Social Maturity	Between groups	2	4661.14	2330.56	6.2	0.01
	Within groups	297	111810.10	376.47		
	Total	299	116471.24			

Interpretation

From the above table it is clear that there is a significant difference of social maturity of Arts and Science college students based on their college type. Hence the null hypothesis is rejected.

Further analysis has been under taken to see group difference in the following table.

Table 12

Showing multiple comparison of the difference of social maturity based on college type.

Factor	College type	Number of students	Mean	SD	SEMD	CR	L.S
	Boys only	90	233.94	20.04	2.113	2.16	0.05
	Girls only	95	240.16	19.1	1.96		
Social	Boys only	90	233.94	20.04	2.113	3.47	0.01
Maturity	Co education	115	243.50	19.16	1.79		
	Girls only	95	240.16	19.1	1.96	1.26	NS
	Co education	115	243.50	19.16	1.79		

Interpretation

The Arts and Science college students for girls only and co-education college are not having significant difference in their social maturity but all other categories are showing significant differences.

Hypothesis-X

There is no significant difference between government and government aided college students on their social intelligence among Arts and Science college students.

Table 13

Showing the difference between social intelligence based on type of management.

Factor	Type of management	Number of students	Mean	SD	SEMD	CR	L.S
Social Intelli-gence	Government	185	95.74	15.10	1.11	1.81	N.S
	Government aided	115	98.87	13.68	1.28		

Interpretation

From the above table it is clear that there is no significant difference between government and government aided college students on their social intelligence among the Arts and Science college students. Hence the null Hypothesis is accepted.

Hypothesis - XI

There is no significant difference between government and government aided college students on their social maturity among Arts and Science college students.

Table 14

Showing the difference between social maturity based on type of management.

Factor	Type of management	Number of students	Mean	SD	SEMD	CR	L.S
Social Maturity	Government	185	237.14	19.75	1.45	2.75	0.01
	Government aided	115	243.50	19.16	1.79		

Interpretation

From the above table, it is clear that there is a significant difference between government and government aided college students on their social maturity among Arts and Science college students. Hence the null hypothesis is rejected.

Hypothesis - XII

There is a significant difference between nuclear and joint family students on their social intelligence among Arts and Science college students.

Table 15

Showing the significant difference between social intelligence based on family type.

Factor	Type of family	Number of students	Mean	SD	SEMD	CR	L.S
Social Intelligence	Nuclear	270	96.38	14.73	0.897	1.99	0.05
	Joint	30	101.97	12.83	2.342		

Interpretation

From the above table, it is clear that there is a significant difference between nuclear and joint family students on their social intelligence among Arts and Science colleges. Hence, the empirical hypothesis is accepted.

Hypothesis - XIII

There is a significant difference between nuclear and joint family students on their social maturity among Arts and Science college students.

Table 16

Showing the difference between social maturity based on type of family.

Factor	Type of family	Number of students	Mean	SD	SEMD	CR	L.S
Social Maturity	Nuclear	270	238.76	20.06	1.22	2.16	0.05
	Joint	30	246.9	14.9	2.72		

Interpretation

From the above table, it is clear that there is a significant difference between nuclear and joint family student on their social maturity among Arts and Science college students. Hence, the empirical hypothesis is accepted.

Hypotheses -XIV

There is a significant difference on social intelligence of Arts and Science college students based on their parental income.

Table 17

Showing the difference of social intelligence based on parental income.

Factor	Source	DF	Sum of	Mean squares	F ratio squares	L.S
Social Intel-ligence	Between groups	2	7020.88	3510.43		
	Within groups	297	56988.92	191.88	18.29	0.01
	Total	299	64009.80			

Interpretation

From the above table, it is clear that there is a significant difference on social intelligence of Arts and Science college students based on their parental income. Hence the empirical hypothesis is accepted.

Further analysis has been undertaken to see the group difference in the following table.

Table 18

Showing multiple comparison of difference of social intelligence based on parental income.

Factor	Parental income	Number of students	Mean	SD	SEMD	CR	L.S
Social Intelligence	<20000	57	89.23	15.19	2.012	2.99	0.01
	20000-50000	150	96.1	14.44	1.18		
	<20000	57	89.23	15.19	2.012	6.22	0.01
	> 50000	93	103.09	11.89	1.23		
	20000-50000	150	96.1	14.44	1.18	3.94	0.01
	>50000	93	103.09	11.89	1.23		

Interpretation

The Arts and Science college students of all the categories are having significant difference in their social intelligence.

Hypothesis: XV

There is a significant difference on social maturity of Arts and Science college students based on their parental income.

Table 19

Showing a difference of social maturity based on parental income.

Factor	Source	DF	Sum of squares	Mean squares	F ratio	L.S
Social Maturity	Between groups	2	14837.84	7418.92	21.68	0.01
	Within groups	297	101633.40	342.2		
	Total	299	116471.24			

Interpretation

From the above table, it is clear that there is a significant difference on the social maturity of Arts and Science college students based on their parental income. Hence the empirical hypothesis is accepted. Further analysis has been undertaken to see group difference in the following table.

Table 20

Showing multiple comparison of social maturity based on parental income.

Factor	Parental income	Number of students	Mean	SD	SEMD	CR	L.S
Social maturity	<20000	57	227.56	20.71	2.74	3.78	0.01
	20000-50000	150	238.94	18.84	1.54		
	<20000	57	227.56	20.71	2.74	6.68	0.01
	> 50000	93	247.97	16.41	1.70		
	20000-50000	150	238.94	18.84	1.54	3.81	0.01
	>50000	93	247.97	16.41	1.70		

Interpretation

The Arts and Science college students of all the categories are having significant difference in their social maturity.

Conclusion

This chapter summarizes the analysis of data, testing of hypothesis description and discussion of the table. A brief report of the research study together with the major findings and conclusion along with their educational implications has been presented in the succeeding chapter.

Summary, Findings & Conclusion

Introduction

In this chapter, after presenting briefly the statement of the problem and the description of the procedure used in the investigation, the findings and the conclusions are presented. In the light of the findings of the present study, a few suggestions have been proposed at the end of the chapter for further research in this field.

Statement of the problem

The problem is titled as, *"A Study of Social Intelligence and Social Maturity among Arts and Science College students"*.

Objectives

1. To find out the level of social intelligence of Arts and Science college students.
2. To find out the level of social maturity of Arts and Science college students.
3. To find out the relationship between social intelligence and social maturity among Arts and Science college students.
4. To find out the significant difference between boys and girls on their social intelligence among Arts and Science colleges.
5. To find out the significant difference between boys and girls on their social maturity among Arts and Science colleges.

6. To find out the significant difference between rural and urban environment on their social intelligence among Arts and Science colleges.
7. To find out the significant difference between rural and urban environment on their social maturity among Arts and Science colleges.
8. To find out the significant difference of social intelligence of Arts and Science college students based on their college type.
9. To find out the significant difference on social maturity of Arts and Science college students based on their college type.
10. To find out the significant difference between government and government aided college students on their social intelligence among Arts and Science College.
11. To find out the significant difference between government and government aided college students on their social maturity among Arts and Science College.
12. To find out the significant difference between nuclear and joint family students on their social intelligence among Arts and Science college students.
13. To find out the significant difference between nuclear and joint family students on their social maturity among Arts and Science college students.
14. To find out the significant difference of social intelligence of Arts and Science college students based on their parental income.
15. To find out the significant difference of social maturity of Arts and Science college students based on their parental income.

Hypotheses

1. The level of social intelligence of Arts and Science college students is moderate in nature.
2. The level of social maturity of Arts and Science college students is moderate in nature.

3. There is a significant relationship between social intelligence and social maturity among Arts and Science college students.
4. There is a significant difference between boys and girls on their social intelligence among Arts and Science Colleges.
5. There is a significant difference between boys and girls on their social maturity among Arts and Science Colleges.
6. There is a significant difference between rural and urban environment on their social intelligence among Arts and Science college students.
7. There is a significant difference between rural and urban environment on their social maturity among Arts and Science college students.
8. There is no significant difference of social intelligence of Arts and Science college students based on their college type.
9. There is no significant difference of social maturity of Arts and Science college students based on their college type.
10. There is no significant difference between government and government aided college students on their social intelligence among Arts and Science college students.
11. There is no significant difference between government and government aided college students on their social maturity among Arts and Science college students.
12. There is a significant difference between nuclear and joint family students on their social intelligence among Arts and Science college students.
13. There is a significant difference between nuclear and joint family students on their social maturity among Arts and Science college students.
14. There is a significant difference on the social intelligence of Arts and Science college students based on their parental income.
15. There is a significant difference on the social maturity of Arts and Science college students based on their parental income.

Sample

IRVIN J.LEHMANN defined, “A sample is a smaller number of elements selected from a population and hopefully representative of that population.

The population consists of students who are studying in arts and science colleges.

The investigator randomly selected 300 students from 3 Arts and Science colleges.

Tools used

The following tools were used,

1. Social intelligence scale by Dr.N.K.Chatha.
2. Social maturity scale by Dr.Nalini Rao

Major findings

The findings arrived at, from the analysis of the data have been presented below,

1. The level of social intelligence among Arts and Science college students is moderate in nature.
2. The level of social maturity among Arts and Science college students is moderate in nature.
3. Students studying Arts and Science College have relationship between social intelligence and social maturity.
4. There is no significant difference between boys and girls studying in Arts and Science College with respect to their social intelligence.
5. There is no significant difference between boys and girls studying in Arts and Science College with respect to their social maturity.
6. There is no significant difference between rural and urban environment Arts and Science college students with respect to their social intelligence.
7. There is no significant difference between rural and urban environment Arts and Science college students with respect to their social maturity.

8. There is no significant difference of social intelligence of Arts and Science college students with respect to their college type.
9. The Arts and Science college students studying girls only and coeducation college are not having significant difference in their social maturity and all other categories are showing significant difference.
10. There is no significant difference between government and government-aided Arts and Science college students with respect to their social intelligence.
11. There is a significant difference between government and government-aided Arts and Science college students with respect to their social maturity.
12. There is a significant difference between nuclear and joint family students on their social intelligence among the Arts and Science Colleges.
13. There is a significant difference between nuclear and joint family students on their social maturity among the Arts and Science Colleges.
14. The Arts and Science college students of all the categories are having significant difference in their social intelligence, based on their parental income.
15. The Arts and Science college students of all the categories are having significant difference in their social maturity, based on their parental income.

Educational implications

Social Intelligence and Social Maturity is an aspect that makes an individual adjusted to the society at large. It is related to the development of the personality of a student. Students studying in Arts and Science colleges are forced to adhere to college regulations as well as social activities. We find that if the students fall in line with the social relationship system and obeying its regulations they may possess a higher social intelligence and social maturity. Therefore for any student social intelligence and social maturity is essential for their daily life.

Hence, the study has a direct impact on the educational practice. The following are some of the major recommendations to be implemented for the social intelligence and social maturity of the students.

- Educators and Administrators should bring about awareness among students to give more importance to develop social intelligence and social maturity.
- Lecturers should provide inspiring leadership to develop social intelligence and social maturity among students.
- Programmes and seminars, which are related to social relationship, are to be arranged in the classroom.

Suggestions for further research

- This study was conducted to 300 Arts and Science college students only. To make the study more comprehensive further studies can be conducted on a larger sample.
- This study could be extended to medical, engineering and technical institutions.
- This study could be extended to professionals also.
- This study is confined to a few variables like, gender, location, type of management and type of family, etc., Other variables like, religion, parental qualification, medium of instruction can also be under taken for further research.

Bibliography

1. Abram M Sulsky, Gary James Schmidt (2002-2003) Silent welfare, Understanding the world of intelligence, Bratteys INC.
2. Abraham Sperling (1967) Definition of social maturity, Vikas publications, NewDelhi.
3. Adhiseshiah, W.T.V. and Pavanasam, R. (1974) Sociology in theory and practice, Shanthi Publishers, NewDelhi, p 38.
4. Agnihotri. L.S (1991) conducted a cross-cultural comparative study between tribal and non-tribal first generation and traditional learners in relation to their social maturity and educational adjustment, M.Phil thesis in Psychology.
5. Adams, Linda (1989) Be Your Best, New York: Putnam.
6. Adler, A. (1939). Social Interest: A Challenge to Mankind, New York: Putnam.
7. Baues Ann Leslie (1995) measured the effect of participation in a peer facilitation project on sixth grades self esteem, social maturity and patterns of social choice. Ph.D, Kent state university.
8. Bhusan.A (1994), conducted a study done on the social maturity across sex and family vocations, Buch, M.B,the educational research, Volume II.

9. Crandall, J. (1981). Theory and Measurement of Social Interest, New York: Columiba University Press.
10. Cuber, J.F. (1995). Sociology, New York: Appleton Century.
11. Cron Bach, L.J. and Gleser, G.C (1954). Review of the study of behaviours; Pcychometric, 19, 329 - 333
12. Downie, N.M and Heath, R.W (1970). Basic statistical methods, New York: Harper and Row.
13. Esther N Goody (1995), "social intelligence and interaction" published by Cambridge University.
14. Harry Elmer Barnes (2004). History and social intelligence, Kessengar publishing.
15. Henry I Garrett (1968), general psychology, Eurasia publishing house Pvt. Ltd., New Delhi, p 88.
16. Ghosh S (1975); A study of the social maturity of Bengali children, applied psychology, Calcutta University.
17. Guilford, J.P. (1967). The Nature of human intelligence, New York: Mcgraw Hill.
18. Guilford, J.P. and Hopener, R. (1971). The analysis of intelligence New York: Mcgraw Hill.
19. Hunt. T. (1928). The measurement of social intelligence, Journel of applied psychology, 12, 317 - 334.
20. Nicholas Humphrrey (2003). The Later Eye social intelligence in Evaluation.
21. Pattraman jumpengern (1986); Social maturity of higher secondary students in Thailand, dissertation abstract international.
22. Piaget, J.1947. The psychology of intelligence.
23. Pintner, R. and Upshall, C.C (1928). Some results of social intelligence.
24. Rai, B.C. (2001), Social psychology, prakashan kentra, lucknow p.29
25. Sarojamma Y.H (1990). A comparative study of reading ability and social maturity of over normal and underachievers of standard V11. Ph. D., edu. Bangalore University.

26. Schacter, Richard, T (1983), sociology, mc graw _ hill, inc. New York, p. 328.
27. Stern, w. (1914). The psychological methods of testing intelligence.
28. Thorndike, E.C (1920). The measurement of intelligence, New York; teachers college Columbia University.
29. Pintner, R. and Upshall, C.C (1928). Some results of social intelligence.

3. Relationship Between Social Intelligence and Life Satisfaction

1

The Problem and its Perspective

Introduction

People who are more satisfied by their lives tend to experience greater physical and psychological health than people who are less satisfied with their lives. From an economic point of view, it is important to know what causes people to be satisfied with their lives. From a psychological perspective, life satisfaction is an important theoretical concept to be understood.

What leads satisfaction with the life? According to the various hypotheses framed, people who have fewer life commitments and demand experiences greater life satisfaction. Thus the person who relaxes on the beach is more satisfied with life than the hurried one but on the other hand, the busy, and involvement in the work creates a satisfied with life. (Bailey and Miller (1998)).

Factors that influence life satisfaction are the availability of social support, personal traits, self esteem, physical health, financial resources, a sense of connectedness, and locus of control. Several studies have explained the relationship between social support and life satisfaction. Most of the literature has indicated that there is a positive relationship exist between social support and life satisfaction.

Life satisfaction has been related to job satisfaction, interpersonal relationship, socio economic status, education, family background and many other variables. All these relationships indicate that life satisfaction is a multidimensional concept. There are various resources found the relationship between life satisfaction and life involvement among the variety of population.

According to cutrona and Altmair (1996) low education and socio economic levels and poor physical health with few social supports have low life satisfaction.

What is social intelligence?

Various individuals are using learned social skills to improve the quality of the life and relationships. Most of human psychological problems were associated with the society. The psychological problems like depression, fear, confusion, anger created by the lack of positive human emotions are critical to the happiness of the individual in the society. So social intelligence is created to bring the skills in to the world of human interaction and relations.

According to E.L. Thorndike (1920) the term intelligence refer the person ability to understand and manage the people and also engage in adopt in social interaction. It also refers the individuals fund of knowledge about the social word (Kihlstrom 1987).

Social intelligence is the ability to understand and manage men and women boys and girls and act wisely with human relations "similarly, Moss and Hunt (1927) defined social intelligence as the "ability to get along with others" Vernon (1933) defined social intelligence as the person's "ability to get along with people in general ability to handle.

Social intelligence is highly combined with the personal and social competence and this is vital for healthy and productive life. Such intelligence is compraised of social competence, social awareness, and social skills. But these are very difficult measuring and various related researchers are proving that there is a direct relationship exist between these skills and the productivity of life (Emmerling 1999)

Definitions of Social Intelligence

According to **Howard Gardener (1983)** Social Intelligence is the capacity to know oneself and to know others is on inalienable a part of the human condition as it is the capacity' to know objects of sounds and it deserves to be investigated not less than these other "less charged" forms.

Vernon (1933) Provided the most wide-ranging definition of social intelligence as the person's "abilities to get along with people in general, social technique or ease in society, knowledge of social matters, susceptibility to stimuli from other members of a group, as well as insight into the temporary moods and underlying personality traits of strangers.

Importance of Social Intelligence

Social intelligence is at the heart of human happiness and emotional comfort. Symptoms of poor social intelligence skills that impact people and organizations include.

1. Half-heartedly listening to others, engaging in mostly surface conversations.
2. Low morale in the workplace.
3. Quickly judging others with no factual basis, often in a critical or demeaning manner.
4. Complaints of racism, sexism, and a hostile work environment.
5. Finding it hard to say "no" to others, even when they may be taking advantage of you.
6. High employee turnover and absenteeism.

Needs of Social Intelligence

Anyone can benefit from social intelligence training and it has been especially successful with the following groups:

1. People in high stress jobs.
2. Single or divorced men and women who would like to find and build a healthy relationship.
3. Senior and mid-level managers
4. Couples experiencing problems in their relationship they would like to better understand and resolve.
5. Workers in a regular contact with the public.
6. Married partners who would like to achieve higher levels of intimacy with one another
7. Organizational trainers and instructors.

Social intelligence training is skills-based, not theoretical. The material is brought to life by skilled trainers who demonstrate problems and illustrate solutions that work in the everyday world.

Factors of Social Intelligence

Patience, co-operativeness, confidence level, sensitivity, recognition of social environment, tactfulness, sense of humour, memory.

a. Patient - calm endurance under stressful situations,
b. Co-operativeness - ability to interact with others in a pleasant way to be able to view matters from all angles.
c. Confidence level - firm trust in one self and one's chances,
d. Sensitivity-to be acutely aware of and responsive,
e. Recognition of social environment - ability to perceive the nature and atmosphere of the existing situation.
f. Tactfulness - delicate perception of the right thing to say or do.
g. Sense of humour - capacity to feel and cause amusement to be able to see the lighter side of life,
h. Memory - ability to remember all relevant issues; names and faces of people.

Life-satisfaction and students

Life satisfaction has been related to job satisfaction, interpersonal relationships, socio economic status, education, family background, and many other variables. All these relationships indicate that life satisfaction is a multidimensional concept. Bailey and Miller (1998) explored the relationship between college student life satisfaction and life involvement.

What leads students to be satisfied with their lives? According to the scarcity hypothesis of life satisfaction, people who have fewer life commitments and demands should experience greater life satisfaction. Thus, the student who relaxes on the beach is more satisfied with life than the harried student involved in volunteer organizations, campus government, and the honor society. On the other hand, according to the expansion hypothesis, the busy, student with involvement in the work is more satisfied with life.

Emotions and life-satisfaction

Depression, positive emotions and cheerfulness are the personality traits that most influence life satisfaction, which was reported Canadian psychology professor Ulrich Schemas of the University of Toronto, and colleagues.

The findings come from four studies and included data from surveys of 136 students at the University of Toronto, the University of Illinois at Urbana-Champaign, and the University of California, Riverside.

The students completed surveys about their personalities and life satisfaction. To get another perspective, the students asked their peers and family members to answer the same questions about the participants' life satisfaction.

Participants rated their life satisfaction and personalities by responding to statements such as, "I tend to be in a good mood", "I tend to be a cheerful and high-spirited person," "I tend to feel hopeless", and "I tend to feel discouraged."

It probably won't surprise many people that depression hinders life satisfaction, positive emotions and cheerfulness.

But you might not have guessed just how powerful depression and cheerfulness are predicting life satisfaction.

In other words, a sunny personality can predict your life satisfaction better than a full social calendar. And depression kills satisfaction more than other grim traits such as anxiety or anger.

'Wouldn't our intuitions predict that somebody who is disposed

to experience more depression, anxiety, and anger has lower life satisfaction than somebody who is only disposed to experience more depression?" ask the researchers.

Individual Differences and life Satisfaction

The notion of individual differences in the inclination to engage in thoughtful activity was proposed early in the history of social psychology and was developed most distinctly through empirical studies on the need for cognition, initially defined by Cohen, Stotland and Wolfe (1955) as a need to understand and make reasonable the experimental world. More recently, Cacioppo and Petty (1982) described the need for cognition as individual differences in the tendency to engage in and enjoy effortful cognitive activity. Individuals high in the need for cognition are highly intrinsically motivated towards thinking, exhibiting a strong tendency to enjoy complex cognitive tasks. Individuals low in the need for cognition are described as "cognitive misers" (Taylor, 1981) who have to be motivated to expend energy on cognitive activities. Cacioppo and Petty (1982) developed a 34-item Need for Cognition Scale (NCS), which was reduced to an 18-item scale (Cacioppo, Petty, and Kao, 1984) in order to increase its administrative efficiency.

Campbell (1981) stated, "the literary image of the crotchety old person, dissatisfied with everything, is not a very realistic picture of older people" (p.203). This pleasant finding may be due to older people being healthier and staying involved in more life domains compared to past reduced to an 18-item scale (Cacioppo, Petty, and Kao, 1984) in order to increase its administrative efficiency.

The lack of significant decrease in life satisfaction across the life span suggests people's ability to adapt to their conditions.

Declines in income and marriage occur across age cohorts in later adulthood, yet, life satisfaction is stable. Some researchers have suggested that these findings serve as evidence that people readjust their goals as they age (Campbell et al., 1976; Rapkin & Fischer, 1992). Continuing with this line of thinking, Ryff (1991) found that older adults, compared with younger people, demonstrate a closer fit between ideal and actual self-perceptions. Brandtstadter and Renner (1990) believe that overcoming adversities is performed either by changing life circumstances to personal preferences (assimilative coping) or by adjusting personal preferences and goals to given situational constraints (accommodative coping) Judging self well-being depends on life satisfaction, satisfaction with important life areas (for instance, work), experiencing many pleasant emotions and moods, and low levels of unpleasant emotional experiences. Once people achieve certain materialistic needs, they become more concerned with self-fulfillment.

Relationship between Social Intelligence and Life Satisfaction

Human society as we know it could not exist without minds and selves, since all its most characteristic features presuppose the possession of minds and selves by its individual members; but its individual members would not possess minds and selves if these had not arisen within or emerged out of the human social process in its lower stages of development-those stages at which it was merely a resultant of, and wholly dependent upon, the physiological differentiations and demands of the individual organisms implicated in it. There must have been such lower stages of the human social process, not only for physiological reasons, but also (if our social theory of the origin and nature of minds and selves is correct) for minds and selves. Consciousness and intelligence, could not otherwise have emerged; because, that is, some sort of an ongoing social process in which human beings were implicated.

Need for the Study

Socially intelligent people are more likely to succeed in

everything they undertake in their life. Unlike what is claimed of I.Q. we can teach and improve in children and in any individual, some crucial social competencies, paying the way for increasing their social intelligence and thus making their life more healthy, enjoyable, successful and satisfied in the coming days. The concept of social intelligence is to be applauded, not because it is totally new, but because it captures the essence of what our children or all of us need to know for living a productive, happy and satisfied life.

Social intelligence as an important factor to get satisfaction in life. Sternberg identified three broad constellations of behaviour which his American interviewers perceived as being intelligent.

1. Practical problem - solving ability; 'keeps our open mind; 'responds thoughtfully to others ideas;
2. Verbal ability; speaks clearly and articulately'; 'is knowledgeable about a field'.
3. Social competence: 'admits mistakes; displays interest in the world at large; 'thinks before speaking and doing'.

Hence the investigator would like to see, if there is a relation between life satisfaction and social intelligence of higher secondary students. The knowledge of the relationship between these variables under the study would help teachers, parents and students to make the needed changes in the system of education.

Scope of the Study

A new concept, 'social intelligence' with its significance even more than one's general intelligence has emerged on the educational scene. It may be defined as one's unitary ability to know, feel and judge emotions in co-operation with a person's thinking process for behaving in a proper way, with the ultimate realization of happiness in himself and in others. In view of its wide significance from the individual as well as social angles, it becomes quite imperative that serious efforts should be made for its proper development, right from the early childhood among the human beings.

Statement of the Problem

Social intelligence and life satisfaction among higher secondary students was chosen as the topic for the present study. Government, Government aided and private schools were selected from Tuticorin District to conduct the study. Data were collected from 300 students (150 boys and 150 girls). In order to test the hypothesis proposed, the investigator statistically analysed the collected data.

Objectives of the Study

1. To relate life satisfaction with that of social intelligence.
2. To find out the relationship between social intelligence with that of educational status of the parent in the case of total sample.
3. To identify associations existing between educational status of the parents and life satisfaction of the total sample.
4. To recognize the impact of type of family on social intelligence and life satisfaction of the total sample.
5. To know the impact of Gender on type of school, social intelligence, life satisfaction and various factors of social intelligence.
6. To interrelate various factors of social intelligence in the case govt., govt. aided and private school students.

Felimitations of the Study

Even though every attempt was made to make the study as precise as possible, certain following limitations have to consider in this study.

1. Since the study has been conducted as part of the course, the investigator has to complete it within the time limitation and also he decided to collect sample randomly in a particular area only, namely Tuticorin District.
2. This study has been restricted only to the higher secondary students in Government, Government Aided and private schools.

3. Samples were collected partly from urban and partly from rural areas. This study was taken to 300 sample.
4. The investigator has taken in to consideration only for two variables namely social intelligence and life satisfaction to conduct the proper way of research.

Inspire of these limitations, the investigator believes that the findings of the present study will be useful to classroom teachers and educator for developing new trends and approaches in the teaching learning process.

Conclusion

The first chapter chiefly concerned with the conceptual frame work of the problem chosen for the study. The discussion on social intelligence and life satisfaction has been presented to high light the connectional position with which this study has been planed and concluded.

2

Review of Related Literature

Introduction

The review of literature promotes a greater understanding of the problem and its crucial aspects. It also provides comparative data on the basis of which to evaluate and to interpret the significance of one's findings. – Mouly (1964)

According to Good (1959) in order to be truly creative and original, one must read extensively and critically as a stimulus of thinking. Therefore careful study is carried out and is presented in this chapter under the following heads.

a. Studies related to social intelligence.
b. Studies related to life satisfaction.

Studies Related to Social Intelligence

The study was under taken by **Buch M.B**. (1960) for assessing the social intelligence of individuals quantitatively and to study the effect of environmental factors as grades and occupational status on social intelligence. The subject for the present study of social intelligence were selected on the basis of certain independent findings supported by the content analysis of the available tests of social intelligence. The sub tests included here were 1. judgement in social situations, 2. Memory for names and faces, 3. observation of human behaviour, 4. recognition of the mental state of the speaker, 5. sense of humour, 6. social introduction.

Ray. T (1972) aimed at developing a test in Bengali for the objective measurement of social intelligence. Final form of the test had eighty items distributed on six subjects corresponding to six different area of human behaviour namely, 1. Judgement of a social situation, 2. observation of human behaviour, 3. Recognition of mental status, 4. Memory for names and faces, 5. Appreciation of humour, 6. Adjustment.

On analyzing the various development trends in social behaviour. Social behaviour was studied in relation to physical, motor, personal language and intellectual development and participation in school activities by **Devi C.L.** (1975), frequency analysis was made for patterning social behaviour into three categories very high, average and low. Discriminating value between the two age groups were calculated for each aspects of social behaviour.

Singhai. S (1986) attempts to study the social interest and attitude of college students and to see how these attitudes will influence their future family organisation. It was found that the social interests and attitude of adolescent students were adequate, mature and stable. It was found that suitable environment influenced development of healthy social interest and attitude of students.

A study was done by **Gabrielsen, Eric** (1992) to examine the role of self monitoring in colleges. A self monitor is an individual who adopts a social orientation so that he / she can manage self presentation. Self monitors are likely to modify their academic choices fit social situations or others expectations. Data were collected using a four-part questionnaire that explored background, a self monitoring scale a personal freedom versus social conformity scale and a friendship scale. Results indicated that self monitoring played a role in selection of college major. However, data also indicated that the direct influence of close friends was not what most persuaded self monitors with regard to choice of major.

A comparative study was undertaken by **Boulon-Diaz, Frances** (1992) on school achievement of the following variables, intelligence, social class, early motor and language development, preschool experience, gender and composition of household. The subjects were 65 children of 9 to 11 years, in grades four to six, in Puerto Rican public schools. They were selected from the sample of 2,200 children used for children revised for the Puerto Rican population. The wise-R Puerto Rico was used to measure IQ.

Mathias, Jane. L (1992) conducted a study on social intelligence with 75 adolescents with mental retardation factor analysis measures of conceptual intelligence adaptive behaviour and social intelligence yielded a practice-interpersonal competence construct. The second study however failed to establish the criterion validity of this construct.

An investigation made by **Nettelbeck Tex** (1992) to define social intelligence, with a total of 125 adolescents with mental retardation, found high to very high inter rater reliability coefficients; moderate to very high internal reliabilities, and moderate to high test-retest reliabilities.

In an experimental study conducted by **Michael, William. B**. (1993) on maximum likelihood, factor analysis determined how accurately each of several hypothesized combinations of first-order and higher order factors reflecting creativity in the social intelligent of 192 high school students described the co-variation in selected sub-matrixes from the total correlation matrix originally analysed.

Laosa, Luis. M (1995) studied that there is a resurgence of scientific and public interest and controversy centering on four interrelated themselves intelligence testing, racial, ethnic and socio-economic differences in measured IQ, genetic and environment influences on abilities and the role of scientific research in social policy.

STUDIES RELATED TO LIFE SATISFACTION

A model of change in Organizational health to improve Quality of life

The paper attempts to develop an empirical model of relationship between organizational health and QOL. Organizational health has been conceptualized as a relatively but quasi-enduring state of physical, mental and social wellbeing of the organization and not merely an absence of strike and lockout. A scale was developed to measure eleven attributes of organizational health. QOL refers to general wellbeingness of employees. GHQ-12 was used to measure wellbeingness of employees. Stratified random sampling was P followed to collect the data from the managers (n=82), supervisors (n=131) and rank and file workers (n=186) of two heavy engineering organizations in private and public sectors. Data were analyzed in terms of multivariate statistics. It was found that each organizational health attribute was positively related with general health. Standardized partial regression analysis revealed that involvement, environmental awareness, creativity and physical health accounted for maximum variances of General health than the other attributes. [Dutta Roy, D. (1991)]

Awareness of external environment, environmental satisfaction and mental health [Chatterjee, A. & Dutta Roy, D (1991]

Samples (n=400) of two heavy engineering organizations were interviewed with a structured questionnaire to study the relationship between two predictors-Awareness of external environment (EA), Environmental satisfaction (ES) and one predicted variable - mental health (MH). Results revealed more accountability of ES than EA to predict MH. However, EA alone failed to predict MH when ES was regressed from EA by standardized partial regression analysis. Possible explanations of the findings were discussed achievement motivation significant relationship existed between achievement motivation and teacher pupil relationship.

Organizational health and life satisfaction: A Path-analytic model

Organizational health and life satisfaction: A Path-analytic model Present study attempts to understand a causal relationship between perceived attributes of organizational health and life satisfaction as a whole. Eleven attributes of organizational health v/ere measured by organizational health scale developed by authors. Life satisfaction was measured by life satisfaction scale (Warr et al., 1979). Data were collected from 400 employees of two heavy engineering organizations in private and public sectors following stratified random sampling. Higher order partial correlation coefficient analysis suggests that each health attribute is casually related with life satisfaction. Path analytic model was proposed lastly to identify some of the strategic variables of organizational health to improve life satisfaction. (Dutta Roy, D. (1992))

Work-Family conflict and Life satisfaction in female Graduate students: Testing mediating and moderating Hypotheses (Treistman, Dana Lynn, (2004)

Most of the research on work-family conflict has examined people working in the paid labor force while simultaneously juggling the roles of paid worker, partner, parent, and homemaker. There is limited research on female graduate students and their experiences of work-family conflict. The goals of the present study were to examine the relationship between work-family conflict (work-to-family conflict and family-to-work conflict) and global life satisfaction, the relationship between work-family conflict and domain-specific satisfactions (family satisfaction and work satisfaction), and the mediators and moderators of these relationships among a sample of female graduate students. Participants included 187 female graduate students. Both work-to-family conflict and family-to-work conflict were hypothesized to be negatively related to domain-specific and global life satisfactions variance to the prediction of achievement. The present experiments tell us that any relationship between motivation and achievement appears to depend on the person's knowledge about their current performance in the area of achievement being measured.

Life satisfaction for people with long-term mental illness

This study attempts to explore those factors and program elements leading to better overall life satisfaction for people with long-term mental illness. The research sample included 88 patients, coming from mental hospitals and a large residential home in Hong Kong. Quality of Life Interview, Perceived Social Support and Sense of Freedom were modified, developed and adopted for data collection purpose. Most of the studied sample suffered from schizophrenia and had been ill for more than twenty years. Results showed that three factors including: number of hospitalization, perceived sense of freedom and social support could explain about one third of the variance in overall life satisfaction of research sample. Based on these findings, a quality of care model, which emphasis on preventing relapse & hospitalization, enhancing sense of freedom and strengthening social support, has been proposed? This quality of care model is suitable for residential home care setting, which aims at promoting the quality of life for people with long-term mental illness.

The relationship between the need for cognition and life satisfaction

The relationship between the need for cognition and life satisfaction was explored among college students. The J8-item short Need for Cognition Scale (NCS; Cacioppo, Petty, & Kao, 1984] and the 5-item Satisfaction with Life Scale (SWLS; Diener, Emmons, Larsen, & Griffin, 1985) were administered to 157 undergraduate university students. Results of a correlation and stepwise multiple regression indicated that currently enrolled students high in the need for cognition expressed greater life satisfaction than students low in the need for cognition. This study supports the hypothesis that the need for cognition is a predictor of life satisfaction among college students.

Successful Aging, Life Satisfaction, and Generativity in Later Life (1995)

Explores meanings for older people attach to successful aging and life satisfaction and to differentiate these concepts, Content analysis of an open ended survey confirmed five features of successful aging: interactions with others, a sense of purpose, self-acceptance, personal growth, and autonomy. Findings suggest generativity contributes to successful aging and remains a vital developmental task in later life. [Fisher – Bradley.J]

Family Resources and Adolescent Family Life Satisfaction in Remarried Family Households (1995)

Examines how family resources and demographic variables relate to adolescent family life satisfaction in remarried family households. Self-report questionnaire data were collected from 95 high school students in remarried families. Showed that flexibility, regularity in household time and routines, and effectiveness in parent communication were significantly related to overall adolescent satisfaction in remarried family households. [Henry, -Carolyn-S .; Lovelace, -Sandra-G.]

Life Satisfaction of Single Middle-Aged Professional Women

Questionnaires were administered to single professional women (n=152) in higher education institutions. Performance on life satisfaction was significantly explained by recourse to the variables of job satisfaction, internal locus of control, regrets regarding life circumstances, sexual satisfaction, and leisure-time activities. [Lewis, -Virginia-G.; Borders, -L.-DiAnne.(1995)]

The Effect of Parental Supportive Behaviors on Life Satisfaction of Adolescent Offspring

Explored effects of parental support on adolescents' life satisfaction in sample of 640 adolescents ages 12 to 16. Three facts of parental support were identified and their effects on child satisfaction were examined. Intrinsic support was strongest predictor of life satisfaction. No differences based on gender of child or parents were found. [Young, -Margaret-H.(1995)]

Validity and Reliability of a Five Dimensional Life Satisfaction Index

The validity of the Five Dimensional Life Satisfaction Index was evaluated with 48 adults with moderate mental retardation.

Results showed reliability of alternate forms and internal consistency, convergent and discriminate validity, and construct validity. [Hawkins, Barbara-A.(1995)]

Conjoint Analyses of the Students' Life Satisfaction Scale and the Piers-Harris Self-Concept Scale

Study investigated the relationships between a children's life satisfaction measure, the Students' Life Satisfaction Scale (SLSS), and a self-concept measure, the Piers-Harris Self-Concept Scale (PHSCS). Analyses demonstrated a strong relationship between the SLSS and one PHSCS subscale, providing support for the construct validity of the SLSS. (RJM) –[Huebner, -E. –Scott (1994)]

The Influence of Separation Orientation on Life Satisfaction in the Elderly

Findings from 154 older adults indicated that separation orientation helped explain differential impact of environmental factors on life satisfaction. Overly dependent subjects were more adversely affected by poor self-rated health and inadequate formal activity than balanced or overly self-sufficient participants. Presence of confidant was associated with higher life satisfaction for overly dependent participants. (Park,-Douglas; Vandenberg,-Brian [1994]).

Family System Characteristics, Parental Behaviors, and Adolescent Family Life Satisfaction

Describes investigation examining adolescents' perceptions of overall family system characteristics, parental behaviors, and demographic factors in relation to adolescent family life satisfaction. Results indicate family bonding, family flexibility, parental support, and adolescent age are positively related to adolescent family life satisfaction, but parental punitiveness is negatively related. [Henry, -Carolyn-S(1994)].

Conclusion

The study of related literature has helped the investigator to have a clear perspective of the problem chosen for the present investigation. The review of the related literature has enabled the investigator to formulate the relevant hypotheses for the present study. Based on this review, a suitable methodology and well planed procedure for the present study is adopted and it is explained in the succeeding chapter.

3

Design of the Study and Method of Investigation

Introduction

This chapter explains the methods and procedures that are used in shaping and framing of hypotheses regarding the social intelligence and life satisfaction of higher secondary school students. This chapter deals with the hypotheses of the present study, tools and techniques used to collect data, validity and reliability of the tools, administration of the tools, pilot study, main study. Statistical techniques used etc.

Statement of the Problem

Social intelligence and Life satisfaction among higher secondary school students was chosen as the topic for the present study. Government, Government Aided and Private Schools were selected to conduct the study. Data were collected from 300 students (150 boys and 150 girls). In order to test the hypothesis proposed, the investigator statistically analyzed the data.

Sample

Total 300 students were taken for the study of which 150 were boys and 150 were girls. The sample was drawn from six schools chosen randomly from higher secondary schools. Out of 300 sample 100 students from Government school, 100 students from Government Aided school and 100 students from Private schools were included.

DISTRIBUTION OF THE TOTAL SAMPLE

Table 1

Type of School	Name of the School	Boys	Girls	Total
Government	Arulmigu Muthumallai Amman Govt. Hr. Sec. School.	25	25	50
	Govt. Hr. Sec. School	25	25	50
	Margoschis Hr. Sec. school.	50	-	50
Government Aided	St. Marks Hr. Sec. School.	-	50	50
	James Memorial Matriculation Hr. Sec. School	25	25	50
Private	Anitha Kumaran Matriculation Hr. Sec. School.	25	25	50
	Total	150	150	300

Objectives

1. To relate life satisfaction with that of social intelligence.
2. To find out the relationship between social intelligence with that of educational status of the parent in the case of total sample.
3. To identify associations existing between educational status of the parents and life satisfaction of the total sample.
4. To recognize the impact of type of family on social intelligence and life satisfaction of the total sample.
5. To know the impact of Gender on type of school, social intelligence, life satisfaction and various factors of social intelligence.
6. To interrelate various factors of social intelligence in the case government, government aided and private school students.

Hypothesis

1. Life satisfaction scores of the students will modify social intelligence.
2. Social intelligence has no impact on education status of the students.
3. Social intelligence does not depend on the type of family.
4. Life satisfaction does not depend on education status.
5. Life satisfaction has no impact with the type of family.
6. Gender plays on important role on life satisfaction of students
7. Gender plays on important role on total score of social intelligence.
8. Gender plays very important role on various factors of social intelligence.
9. Various factors of social intelligence are related to each other in government school.
10. Different factors of social intelligence are related to each other in the case of government aided school.
11. Various factors of social intelligence are interrelated among themselves in private school.

Tools and Techniques

To verify the framed hypotheses, the following tools and techniques were used in the present investigation.

1. Social intelligence scale by Dr. N.K. Chadha
2. Life Satisfaction Scale by Dr. Promila Singh.

SOCIAL INTELLIGENCE SCALE

Description

This test consists of 54 items and 12 eminent persons constructed by **Dr.N.K. Chadha.** This tool deals with 6 factors of social intelligence. They are patience, confidence, cooperativeness, sensitivity, sense of humour and recognition of social environment.

Administration

The social intelligence tool is constructed with simple sentences. The following instructions were given to the subjects before administrating the test. "There are some statements regarding the way in which we behave, feel and act. We want your first response. Please try to make your best possible answer honestly and sincerely. Read and understand each question properly and then put your mark on any cell against every statement on the answer sheet by making the sign of cross (X) please do not omit any question. In part I read the following statements carefully and among the three responses given for each of them, pick up the one which seems to you to the most likely way in which you would respond. You are to choose only one response from a, b and c, and mark a cross (X) on the appropriate cell on the answer - sheet. In part II select the word that most accurately describes the mental state of the person making the statement. Cross out (X) the correct answer on the answer - sheet. In part III there are some statements regarding the way you behave and act. Each statement has a forced choice response of either 'yes' or 'No', try and decide whether 'Yes' or 'No' represents your usual way of behaviour and acting. If yes, cross out (X) the cell below 'Yes' and if no, then cross out (X) the cell below 'No'. In part IV list of incomplete jokes are given. Against them, there are three choices with which to complete the joke. You are to select and cross out (X) the choice you consider to be the most humorous. In part V list of eminent persons are given.

Scoring Procedure

In the case of the first four dimensions (patience, cooperativeness, confidence and sensitivity) scores of 1,2 and 3 were given to three response alternatives. For e.g., in the confidence dimension a score of 3 would indicate a high degree of confidence, a score of 1 a lack of confidence and a core of 2 would reveal moderate confidence. In the other two dimensions (Sense of Humour and Recognition of Social Environment) one of three alternatives given is the appropriate response. This response when given was allotted of scores of 1. In the case of the 'Tactfulness' dimension the responses were in the form of 'Yes' or 'No'. The appropriate response was awarded a score of '1'. The last dimension that of Memory was scored '1' or '0' depending on whether or not the subject's response was 'right' or 'wrong'.

LIFE SATISFACTION SCALE

Description

This test consists of 35 items constructed by Dr. Mrs. Promila Singh. She construct a life satisfaction scale based on the following dimensions,

(a) Taking Pleasure in everybody activities

(b) considering life meaningful,

(c) holding a positive self-image,

(d) having a happy and optimistic outlook,

(e) feeling success in achieving goals.

The present scale was constructed by considering the above five dimensions of life satisfaction.

Administration

This questionnaire consists of simple statement, which expresses the different way in which students think, feel and behavior in their life situation. They were asked to indicate their responses for each statement by putting a tick (V) against any one of the five boxes always, often, sometimes, seldom and never and which are respectively scored as 5 4, 3, 2 and 1.

Scoring Procedure

The scale consists of 35 items each item is to be rated on the five-point scale always, often, sometimes, seldom and never and which are respectively scored as 5, 4, 3, 2 and 1 . The items relate to the individuals all-round activities and thus give a global picture of ones life satisfaction level. The higher the score on the life satisfaction scale for the higher will be the level of life satisfaction.

Interpreting the Score of Life Satisfaction

Table 2

Satisfaction level	Range of scores
High	136-175
Average	81-135
Low	35-80

Pilot Study

A pilot study was carried out to know suitability of the time required to administer the test of social intelligence and life satisfaction and to establish the reliability and validity of the tools. So students were selected for the pilot study. The tools were given based on data reliability and validity of the social intelligence questionnaire and life satisfaction questionnaire were calculated for the present study.

ESTABLISHING RELIABILITY AND VALIDITY OF THE TOOLS USED IN THE STUDY

Reliability of Social Intelligence Scale

In order to establish the reliability of the social intelligence scale, the split half method was used. The reliability of social intelligence scale was found to be **0.817**. Hence social intelligence scale is considered as a reliable tool.

Validity of Social Intelligence Scale

The index of validity which is the square root of reliability was found to be **0.9**. Hence social intelligence scale selection for the study was considered to have high validity.

Reliability of Life Satisfaction Scale

The test-retest reliability computed after a lapse of 8 weeks turned out to be **0.91**.

Validity of Life Satisfaction Scale

To determine validity of the life satisfaction scale co-efficient of correlation between the scale of Alam and Singh (1971) was computed and the co-efficient of correlation was found to be **0.83**. The scale also possesses face and content validity since experts judged each item.

Statistical Techniques

Suitable descriptive and inferential statistical techniques were used in the interpretation of the data to draw out a more meaningful picture of results from the collected data.

Life Satisfaction and total social intelligence scores were classified as low, moderate and high.

In the present study the following statistical measures were used.

Arithmetic Mean (x)

Mean is the simplest measures of central tendency, which is calculated by adding all the scores and dividing the sum by the number of scores.

Mean x = A+ ———

$$\left[\frac{\sum fd}{\sum f}\right] \times \text{i}$$

Where,

A = Assumed Mean

d = Deviation from the assumed mean.

f = Frequency

i = Class interval.

Standard Deviation

The standard deviation is defined as the square root of mean of the squares of the items taken from the arithmetic mean of the distribution.

= i

Where,

i	=	Class Interval
f	=	Frequency.
N	=	Total No. of Frequencies
d	=	Deviation.

Karl Pearson's Correlation Coefficient

$$\square = \frac{N\sum dxdy - \sum dx\sum dy}{\sqrt{\left[N\sum dx^2 - (\sum dx)^2\right]\left[N\sum dy^2 - (\sum dy)^2\right]}}$$

Where dx	=	Deviation of continuous values of the variable X from the assumed mean A.
dy	=	Deviation of continuous values of the variable Y from the assumed mean B.
N	=	Number of Pairs
Σdx^2	=	Summation of deviations of continuous values of the variable X.
Σdy^2	=	Summation of Deviations of continuous values of the variable Y.
Σdx^2	=	Summation of the square of deviations of continuous values of the variable X.
Σdy^2	=	Summation of the square of deviations of continuous values of the variable Y.
$\Sigma dxdy$	=	Summation of the product of deviations of continuous values of variables X and Y.

Chi-Square test (x^2)

$$= \frac{\sum (f_0 - f_a)^2}{f_e}$$

Here f_e = $\frac{\text{Row Total x Column Total}}{\text{Total Frequency}}$

Where f_0 = Observed Frequency

f_e = Expected Frequency

Degrees of freedom = (row-1) (column-1)

't' Test

a. If mean and standard deviation are given the 't' value is calculated from the following formula.

't' value = $\frac{X_1 X_2}{S.E_M}$

Here S.EM =

b. If Correlation coefficient is given, the 't' value is calculated by using the following formula.

't' value =

Where, n is the total number of samples and y is the correlation coefficient.

If the number of group is 2 then degrees of freedom is equal to $(n_1-1)+(n_2-1)$.

Where n_1 and n_2 are the no. of sample of group 1 and 2.

Conclusion

This chapter outlines the design of the present study, the procedure followed and the nature of the sample. It describes the hypotheses to be tested, the tools to be used and the methods of administration and scoring. The method of investigation designed was found to be quite appropriate and effective for the study.

4

Analysis and Interpretation of Data

Introduction

This chapter highlights the analysis of the data obtained regarding the variables of the present study social intelligence and life satisfaction among higher secondary school students using appropriate techniques and verifying hypothesis framed for the present study. The findings were interpreted and discussed in the light of findings of other research studies.

Hypothesis-1

Life satisfaction scores of the students will modify social intelligence.

Table 1

To correlate social intelligence with that of life satisfaction of boys & girls of Private School

Variables	Gender	No	Mean	S.D	'r'	't'	L.S
Social	Boys	50	99.1	9.26	0.279	2.013	0.05
intelligence			126.28	18.32			
& life			106.46	7.6			
satisfaction	Girls	50	38.7	12.177	0.3339	2.5	0.01

Table 2

To correlate social intelligence with that of life satisfaction of boys & girls of Government Aided Schools

Variables	Gender	No	Mean	S.D	'r'	't'	L.S
	Boys	50	94.78	8.65	0.229	1.629	N.S
Social intelligence			131.7	14.66			
& life satisfaction	Girls	50	103.5	8.39	0.094	0.65	N.S
			138.72	15.55			

Table 3

To correlate social intelligence with that of life satisfaction of boys & girls of Government Aided Schools

Variables	Gender	No	Mean	S.D	'r'	't'	L.S
	Boys	50	101.62	7.07	0.321	2.14	0.05
Social intelligence			140.32	17.04			
& life satisfaction	Girls	50	102.58	5.97	0.011	0.07	N.S
			136.78	13.36			

The tables 1 to 3 and from Fig. E it is understood that the calculated 'r' values were greater than that of table 'r' values in the case of boys & girls of Private School and boys of Government School. So hypothesis was accepted in these cases and proved life satisfaction scores of the students modified social intelligence scores. Where as in the case of boys and girls of Government Aided School and girls of Government School, the calculated 'r' values were less than that of table 'r' values. Hence hypothesis was rejected in these cases.

Hypothesis-2

Social intelligence has no impact on Education status of the students.

Table 4

Chi square test between Education status and Social Intelligence of boys and girls of Private School

Variables	Gender	No	D.F	χ^2	L.S
Social Intelligence Vs	Boys	50	4	2.o3	N.S
Education Status	Girls	50	4	5.05	N.S

Table 5

Chi square test between Education status and Social Intelligence of boys and girls of Government Aided School

Variables	Gender	No	D.F	$\chi2$	L.S
Social Intelligence Vs	Boys	50	4	8.4	N.S
Education Status	Girls	50	4	1.64	N.S

Table 6

Chi square test between Education status and Social Intelligence of boys and girls of Government School

Variables	Gender	No	D.F	χ^2	L.S
Social Intelligence Vs	Boys	50	4	4.29	N.S
Education Status	Girls	50	4	2.41	N.S

The tables 4 to 6 shows that the calculate chi-square value were less than that of table chi-square values. Hence the hypothesis was accepted and proved that intelligence has no impact on education status of the students in the case of boys and girls from Government, Government aided & Private Schools.

Hypothesis - 3

Social intelligence does not depend on the type of family of students.

Table 7

To associate Social Intelligence with that of family status of boys and girls of Private School

Variables	Gender	No	D.F	χ^2	L.S
Social Intelligence Vs	Boys	50	2	1.87	N.S
Education Status	Girls	50	2	2.49	N.S

Table 8

To associate Social Intelligence with that of family status of boys and girls of Government Aided School

Variables	Gender	No	D.F	χ^2	L.S
Social Intelligence Vs	Boys	50	2	4.12	N.S
Education Status	Girls	50	2	0.56	N.S

Table 9

To associate Social Intelligence with that of family status of boys and girls of Government School

Variables	Gender	No	D.F	χ^2	L.S
Social Intelligence Vs	Boys	50	2	1.72	N.S
Education Status	Girls	50	2	0.75	N.S

The tables 7 to 9 shows that the calculated chi-square values were less than that of table chi-square values. Hence the hypothesis was accepted and proved that intelligence did not depend upon the type of family of the students in the case of boys and girls from government, government aided and Private Schools.

Hypothesis-4

"Life satisfaction does not depend on Education status".

Table 10

Chi square test between Education status and Life Satisfaction of boys and girls of Private School

Variables	Gender	No	D.F	χ^2	L.S
Life Intelligence Vs	Boys	50	4	1.02	N.S
Education Status	Girls	50	4	5.31	N.S

Table 11

Chi square test between Education status and Life Satisfaction of boys and girls of Government Aided School

Variables	Gender	No	D.F	χ^2	L.S
Life Intelligence Vs	Boys	50	4	13.2	0.05
Education Status	Girls	50	4	8.5	N.S

Table 12

Chi square test between Education status and Life Satisfaction of boys and girls of Government School

Variables	Gender	No	D.F	χ^2	L.S
Life Intelligence Vs	Boys	50	4	1.73	N.S
Education Status	Girls	50	4	4.93	N.S

The tables 10 to 12 shows that the calculate chi-square values were less than that of table chi-square values. Hence the hypothesis was accepted and proved that life satisfaction does not depend on education status of the students in the case of boys and girls from Private, Government School and girls from Government Aided School where as in the case of boys of Government Aided School. The calculated chi-square values were greater than the table chi-square values. Hence hypothesis was rejected in these cases.

Hypothesis-5

Life satisfaction has no impact on the type of family.

Table 13

Chi square test between Life Satisfaction and family status boys and girls of Private School

Variables	Gender	No	D.F	χ^2	L.S
Life Intelligence Vs	Boys	50	2	0.71	N.S
Education Status	Girls	50	2	0.48	N.S

Table 14

Chi square test between Life Satisfaction and family status of boys and girls of Government Aided School

Variables	Gender	No	D.F	χ^2	L.S
Life Intelligence Vs	Boys	50	2	0.82	N.S
Education Status	Girls	50	2	3.27	N.S

Table 15

Chi square test between Life Satisfaction and of family status boys and girls of Government School

Variables	Gender	No	D.F	χ^2	L.S
Life Intelligence Vs	Boys	50	2	2.73	N.S
Education Status	Girls	50	2	0.94	N.S

The tables 13 to 15 show that the calculated chi-square values were less than that of table chi-square values. Hence the hypothesis was accepted and proved that life satisfaction had no impact on the type of family of the students in the case of boys and girls from government, government aided and Private Schools.

Hypothesis 6

Gender plays an important role on life satisfaction of students.

Table 16

To differentiate life satisfaction of boys & girls of Private Schools

Variables	Gender	No	Mean	S.D.	C.R	L.S.
Life Satisfaction	Boys	50	126.28	18.32	6.9	0.01
	Girls	50	138.7	12.177		

Table 17

To differentiate life satisfaction of boys & girls of Government Aided Schools

Variables	Gender	No	Mean	S.D.	C.R	L.S.
Life Satisfaction	Boys	50	131.7	14.66	2.32	0.05
	Girls	50	138.72	15.55		

Table 18

To differentiate life satisfaction of boys & girls of Government Schools

Variables	Gender	No	Mean	S.D.	C.R	L.S.
Life Satisfaction	Boys	50	140.32	17.04	1.44	NS
	Girls	50	136.78	13.36		

The tables 16 to 18 shows that the calculated CR value are greater than the table CR values. Hence the hypothesis was accepted and proved that Gender played an important role on life satisfaction of student in the case of Private School and Government Aided School, where as in the case of Government School the calculated CR value were less than that of table CR values. Hence the hypothesis was rejected in these cases.

Hypothesis-7

Gender plays an important role on total score of social intelligence.

Table 19

To differentiate the total score of social intelligence of boys & girls of Private School

Variables	Gender	No	Mean	S.D.	C.R	L.S.
Social intelligence	Boys	50	99.1	9.26	7.36	0.01
	Girls	50	106.46	7.6		

Table 20

To differentiate the total score of social intelligence of boys & girls of Government aided school

Variables	Gender	No	Mean	S.D.	C.R	L.S.
Social intelligence	Boys	50	94.78	8.65	5.11	0.01
	Girls	50	103.5	8.39		

TABLE 21

To differentiate the total score of social intelligence of boys & girls of Government School

Variables	Gender	No	Mean	S.D.	C.R	L.S.
Social intelligence	Boys	50	101.62	7.07	0.692	N.S
	Girls	50	102.58	5.97		

The tables 19 to 21 show that clearly that the calculated CR values were greater than that of the table CR values. Hence the hypothesis was accepted and proved that Gender played an important role on total score of social intelligence of student in the case of Private School and Government Aided School, where as in the case of Government School the calculated CR value were less than that of table CR values. Hence the hypothesis was rejected in these cases.

Table 22 and Fig. F show that the calculated CR values were greater than that of table CR values. Hence the hypothesis was accepted and proved that Gender played very important role on patience factors of social intelligence in the case of boys and girls of Private School and Government Aided Schools. Where as in the case of Government School, the hypothesis was rejected and proved that Gender did not play important role on patience factors of social intelligence.

Hypothesis-8

Gender plays an important role on various factors of social intelligence of the total sample.

Table 22

To differentiate patience between boys and girls of Private, Government aided and Government School

Variable	Type of School	Gender	No	Mean	S.D	C.R	L.S
	Private	Boys	50	18.274	3.516	3.9	0.01
		Girls	50	20.5	2.10		
	Government	Boys	50	17.74	2.7	13.7	0.01
Patience	Aided	Girls	50	19.98	2.645		
	Government	Boys	50	19.18	2.1	0.769	N.S
		Girls	50	19.44	2.06		

Table 23

To differentiate co-operatives between boys and girls of Private, Government aided and Government School

Variable	Type of School	Gender	No	Mean	S.D	C.R	L.S
	Private	Boys	50	25.215	3.46	2.15	0.05
		Girls	50	26.58	2.81		
CO-	Government	Boys	50	24.54	2.8	1.607	N.S
operative	Aided	Girls	50	26.46	3.55		
	Government	Boys	50	26.96	2.42	0.264	N.S
		Girls	50	26.82	1.97		

The table 23 and Fig. G show that the calculated CR values were greater than that of table CR values. Hence the hypothesis was accepted and proved that gender played very important role on co-operativeness factors of social intelligence in the case of boys and girls of Private School. Where as in the case of boys and girls of Government Aided School and Government School, the hypothesis was rejected and proved that gender did not played important role on co-operativeness factors of social intelligence.

Table 24

To differentiate confidence between boys & girls of Private, Government aided and Government Schools

Variable	Type of School	Gender	No	Mean	S.D	C.R	L.S
	Private	Boys	50	18.901	2.5	3.15	0.01
		Girls	50	20.62	1.75		
Confidence	Government Aided	Boys	50	18.64	2.94	2.88	0.01
		Girls	50	20.08	2.2		
	Government	Boys	50	20.46	2.2	4.08	0.01
		Girls	50	22.22	1.95		

The table 24 and Fig. H show that the calculated CR values were greater than that of table CR values. Hence the hypothesis was accepted and proved that Gender played very important role on confidence factors of social intelligence in the case of boys and girls of Private School, Government Aided School and Government School.

Table 25

To differentiate sensitivity between boys & girls of private, Government aided and Government School

Variable	Type of School	Gender	No	Mean	S.D	C.R	L.S
	Private	Boys	50	20.529	2.6	1.03	NS
		Girls	50	21.26	2.04		
Sensitivity	Government Aided	Boys	50	19.48	2.22	0.99	NS
		Girls	50	20.66	2.84		
	Government	Boys	50	20.72	2.3	0.610	NS
		Girls	50	20.98	1.94		

The table 25 and Fig. I show that the calculated CR values were greater than that of table CR values. Hence the hypothesis was rejected and proved that Gender did not play important role on sensitivity factors of social intelligence in the case of Private School, Government Aided School and Government School.

Table 26

To differentiate Recognition of Social Environment between boys & girls of Private, Government aided and Government School

Variable	Type of School	Gender	No	Mean	S.D	C.R	L.S
	Private	Boys	50	0.84	0.7	1.33	NS
		Girls	50	0.62	0.7		
Recogniton of Social Environment	Government Aided	Boys	50	1.06	0.7	27.5	0.01
		Girls	50	0.64	0.7		
	Government	Boys	50	0.94	0.7	0.133	NS
		Girls	50	0.92	0.7		

The table 26 and Fig. J show that the calculated CR values were greater than that of table CR values. Hence the hypothesis was accepted and proved that Gender played very important role on recognition of social environment factors of social intelligence in the case of boys and girls of Government Aided School. Where as in the case of PRIVATE SCHOOL and Government School, the hypothesis was rejected and proved that Gender did not play important role on recognition of social environment factors of social intelligence.

Table 27

To differentiate tactfulness between boys & girls of Private, Government aided and Government School

Variable	Type of School	Gender	No	Mean	S.D	C.R	L.S
	Private	Boys	50	3.627	0.87	3.16	0.01
		Girls	50	4.28	1.08		
Tactfulness	Government Aided	Boys	50	3.46	1.09	0.542	NS
		Girls	50	3.38	1.12		
	Government	Boys	50	3.88	1.13	2.39	0.05
		Girls	50	4.4	1.04		

The table 27 and fig. K show that the calculated CR values were greater than that of table CR values. Hence the hypothesis was accepted and proved that Gender played very important role on tactfulness in the case of boys and girls of Government School and Government School. Where as in the case of boys and girls of

Government Aided School, the hypothesis was rejected and proved that Gender did not play important role on tactfulness factors of social intelligence.

Table 28

To differentiate sense of humour between boys and girls of private, Government aided and Government School

Variable	Type of School	Gender	No	Mean	S.D	C.R	L.S
Sense of Humor	Private	Boys	50	3.549	1.269	2.09	0.05
		Girls	50	3.68	1.7		
	Government Aided	Boys	50	3.24	1.17	0.36	NS
		Girls	50	3.16	1.03		
	Government	Boys	50	2.96	0.9	1.29	NS
		Girls	50	3.18	0.8		

The table 28 and Fig. L show that the calculated CR values were greater than that of table CR values. Hence the hypothesis was accepted and proved that Gender played very important role on sense of humour factors of social intelligence in the case of boys and girls of Private School. Where as in the case of Government Aided School and Government School, the hypothesis was rejected and proved that Gender did not play important role on sense of humour factors of social intelligence.

Table 29

To differentiate memory between boys and girls of private, government aided and Government School

Variable	Type of School	Gender	No	Mean	S.D	C.R	L.S
Memory	Private	Boys	50	8.372	2.16	1.76	NS
		Girls	50	8.92	0.16		
	Government Aided	Boys	50	6.62	1.44	6.0	0.01
		Girls	50	8.54	1.71		
	Government	Boys	50	5.96	1.33	0.67	NS
		Girls	50	5.81	0.82		

The table 29 and Fig. M show that the calculated CR values were greater than that of table CR values. Hence the hypothesis was accepted and proved that Gender played very important role on memory factors of social intelligence in the case of boys and girls of Government Aided School. Where as in the case of Private School and Government School, the hypothesis was rejected and proved that Gender did not play important role on memory factors of social intelligence.

Hypotheses-9

Various factors of social intelligence are related to each other of Government School.

Table 30

To correlate Patience with that of Co-operativeness, Confidence, Sensitivity, Recognition of Social Environment, Tactfulness, sense of Humour and Memory of Government of School Boys

Variables	No	Mean	S.D	'r'	't'	L.S
Patience Vs	50	19.18	2.1	0.189	1.33	N.S
Cooperativeness	50	26.96	2.42			
Patience Vs	50	19.18	2.1	0.484	3.83	0.05
Confidence	50	20.46	2.2			
Patience Vs	50	19.18	2.1	0.252	1.80	N.S
Sensitivity	50	20.72	2.3			
Patience Vs	50	19.18	2.1			
Recognition of Social Environment	50	0.94	0.8	0.005	0.03	N.S
Patience Vs	50	19.18	2.1	0.025	0.17	N.S
Tactfulness	50	3.88	1.13			
Patience Vs	50	19.18	2.1	-0.14	0.97	N.S
Sense of Humour	50	2.96	0.9			
Patience Vs	50	19.18	2.1	0.141	0.98	N.S
Memory	50	5.96	1.33			

Table 31

To correlate Patience with that of Co-operativeness, Confidence, Sensitivity, Recognition of Social Environment, Tactfulness, sense of Humour and Memory of Government of School Girls

Variables	No	Mean	S.D	'r'	't'	L.S
Patience Vs	50	19.44	2.06	0.375	2.80	0.01
Cooperativeness	50	26.82	1.97			
Patience Vs	50	19.44	2.06	0.289	2.09	0.05
Confidence	50	22.22	1.95			
Patience Vs	50	19.44	2.06	0.363	2.69	0.01

Sensitivity	50	20.98	1.94			
Patience Vs	50	19.44	2.06	0.228	1.62	N.S
Recognition of Social Environment	50	0.92	0.7			
Patience Vs	50	19.44	2.06	0.035	0.24	N.S
Tactfulness	50	4.4	1.04			
Patience Vs	50	19.44	2.06	0.21	1.48	N.S
Sense of Humour	50	3.18	0.9			
Patience Vs	50	19.44	2.06	0.076	0.52	N.S
Memory	50	5.81	0.82			

From the tables 30 to 43 shows the correlation values among different factors of social intelligence in the case of Government School, tables 30 and 31 when patience was correlated with confidence the calculated 'r' value were greater than that of table 'r' values. So hypothesis was accepted and proved that patience and confidence were, interrelated in the case of Government School boys and girls. When patience was related with co-operatives and sensitivity it was found to be significant in Government School Girls, where as other factor were correlated with patience it was found to be not significant in the case of boys and girls of Government School.

Table 32

To correlate Co-operativeness with that of Confidence, Sensitivity, Recognition of Social Environment, Tactfulness, Sense of humour and Memory of Government School Boys

Variables	No	Mean	S.D	'r'	't'	L.S
Cooperativeness Vs	50	26.96	2.42	0.32	2.33	0.05
Confidence	50	20.46	2.2			
Cooperativeness Vs	50	26.96	2.42	0.316	2.43	0.05
Sensitivity	50	20.72	2.3			
Cooperativeness Vs	50	26.96	2.42			
Recognition of Social Environment	50	0.94	0.8	-0.309	2.25	0.05
Cooperativeness Vs	50	26.96	2.42	0.183	1.29	0.05
Tactfulness	50	3.88	1.13			
Cooperativeness Vs	50	26.96	2.42	0.025	0.17	N.S
Sense of Humour	50	2.96	0.9			
Cooperativeness Vs	50	26.96	2.42	0.049	0.33	N.S
Memory	50	5.96	1.33			

Table 33

To correlate Co-operativeness with that of Confidence, Sensitivity, Recognition of Social Environment, Tactfulness, Sense of humour and Memory of Government School Girls

Variables	No	Mean	S.D	'r'	't'	L.S
Cooperativeness Vs	50	26.82	1.97	0.317	2.31	0.05
Confidence	50	22.22	1.95			
Cooperativeness Vs	50	26.82	1.97	0.286	2.06	0.05
Sensitivity	50	20.98	1.94			
Cooperativeness Vs	50	26.82	1.97			
Recognition of Social Environment	50	0.92	0.7	0.006	0.04	N.S
Cooperativeness Vs	50	26.82	1.97	0.133	0.92	N.S
Tactfulness	50	4.4	1.04			
Cooperativeness Vs	50	26.82	1.97	0.149	1.04	N.S
Sense of Humour	50	3.18	0.9			
Cooperativeness Vs	50	26.82	1.97	0.061	0.42	N.S
Memory	50	5.81	0.82			

The tables 32 and 33 shows that co-operativeness was correlated with confidence and sensitivity, the calculated 'r' values were greater than that of table values. So hypothesis was accepted and proved that cooperativeness was related with confidence and sensitivity in the case of Government School boys & girls. When the cooperativeness was related with recognition of school environment and tactfulness it was found to be significant in Government School boys. Whereas other factors were correlated with cooperativeness it was found not to be significant in the case of boys and girls of Government Schools.

Table 34

To correlate Confidence with that of Sensitivity, Recognition of Social Environment, Tactfulness, Sense of humour and Memory of Government School boys

Variables	No	Mean	S.D	'r'	't'	L.S
Confidence Vs	50	20.46	2.2	0.258	1.85	N.S
Sensitivity	50	20.72	2.3			
Confidence Vs	50	20.46	2.2			
Recognition of Social Environment	50	0.94	0.8	0.04	0.27	N.S
Confidence Vs	50	20.46	2.2	0.12	0.83	N.S
Tactfulness	50	3.88	1.13			

Confidence Vs	50	20.46	2.2	0.086	0.59	N.S
Sense of Humour	50	2.96	0.9			
Confidence Vs	50	20.46	2.2	0.234	1.66	N.S
Memory	50	5.96	1.33			

Table 35

To correlate Confidence with that of Sensitivity, Recognition of Social Environment, Tactfulness, Sense of Humour and Memory of Government School Girls

Variables	No	Mean	S.D	'r'	't'	L.S
Confidence Vs	50	22.22	1.95	0.168	1.18	N.S
Sensitivity50	20.98	1.94				
Confidence Vs	50	22.22	1.95			
Recognition of Social Environment	50	0.92	0.7	0.027	0.18	N.S
Confidence Vs	50	22.22	1.95	0.135	0.94	N.S
Tactfulness	50	4.4	1.04			
Confidence Vs	50	22.22	1.95	0.044	0.30	N.S
Sense of Humour	50	3.18	0.8			
Confidence Vs	50	22.22	1.95	0.046	0.31	N.S
Memory	50	5.81	0.82			

The tables 34 and 35 shows that when confidence was correlated with other factors, the calculated 'r' values were lesser than that of table 'r' values. So hypothesis was rejected and proved that confidence and various factors of social intelligence were not related in the case of Government School boys and girls.

Table 36

To correlate Sensitivity with that of Recognition of Social Environment, Tactfulness, Sense of humour and Memory of Government School boys

Variables	No	Mean	S.D	'r'	't'	L.S
Sensitivity Vs	50	20.72	2.3			
Recognition of Social Environment	50	0.94	0.8	0.012	0.08	N.S
Sensitivity Vs	50	20.72	2.3	0.178	1.25	N.S
Tactfulness	50	3.88	1.13			
Sensitivity Vs	50	20.72	2.3	0.119	0.83	N.S
Sense of Humour	50	2.96	0.9			
Sensitivity Vs	50	20.72	2.3	0.194	1.37	N.S
Memory	50	5.96	1.33			

Table 37

To correlate Sensitivity with that of Recognition of Social Environment, Tactfulness, Sense of humour and Memory of Government School Girls

Variables	No	Mean	S.D	'r'	't'	L.S
Sensitivity Vs	50	20.98	1.94			
Recognition of Social Environment	50	0.92	0.7	0.119	0.83	N.S
Sensitivity Vs	50	20.98	1.94	0.084	0.58	N.S
Tactfulness	50	4.4	1.04			
Sensitivity Vs	50	20.98	1.94	0.348	2.57	0.01
Sense of Humour	50	3.18	0.8			
Sensitivity Vs	50	20.98	1.94	0.113	0.78	N.S
Memory	50	5.81	0.82			

The tables 36 and 37 shows that when sensitivity was correlated with sense of humour, the calculated r values were greater than that of table 'r' values. So hypothesis was proved the sensitivity and sense of humour were interrelated in the case of Government School girls. When the sensitivity was related with other factors it was not found to be significant in the case of boys and girls of Government School.

Table 38

To correlate Recognition of Social Environment with tactfulness, Sense of humour and Memory of Government School boys

Variables	No	Mean	S.D	'r'	't'	L.S
Recognition of Social Environment Vs	50	0.94	0.8	0.035	0.24	N.S
Tactfulness	50	3.88	1.13			
Recognition of Social Environment Vs	50	0.94	0.8	0.054	0.37	N.S
Sense of Humour	50	2.96	0.9			
Recognition of Social Environment Vs	50	0.94	0.8	0.002	0.01	N.S
Memory	50	5.96	1.33			

The tables 38 and 39 shows that when recognition of social environment was correlated with sense of humour, tactfulness and memory the calculated r values were less than that of table r values. It was found not to be significant. The hypothesis was rejected in these cases of boys and girls of Government School.

Table 39

To correlate Recognition of Social Environment with tactfulness, Sense of humour and Memory of Government School girls

Variables	No	Mean	S.D	'r'	't'	L.S
Recognition of Social Environment Vs	50	0.92	0.7	0.143	1.00	N.S
Tactfulness	50	4.4	1.04			
Recognition of Social Environment Vs	50	0.92	0.7	0.07	0.48	N.S
Sense of Humour	50	3.18	0.8			
Recognition of Social Environment Vs	50	0.92	0.7	0.01	0.06	N.S
Memory	50	5.81	0.82			

Table 40

To correlate Tactfulness with Sense of humour and Memory of Government School boys

Variables	No	Mean	S.D	'r'	't'	L.S
Tactfulness Vs	50	3.88	1.13	0.273	1.96	N.S
Sense of Humour	50	2.96	0.9			
Tactfulness Vs	50	3.88	1.13	0.257	1.84	N.S
Memory	50	5.96	1.33			

Table 41

To correlate Tactfulness with Sense of humour and Memory of Government School Girls

Variables	No	Mean	S.D	'r'	't'	L.S
Tactfulness Vs	50	4.4	1.04	0.0289	0.20	N.S
Sense of Humour	50	3.18	0.8			
Tactfulness Vs	50	4.4	1.04	0.108	0.75	N.S
Memory	50	5.81	0.82			

The tables 40 and 41 shows that when tactfulness was correlated with sense of humour and memory the calculated 'r' values were less than that of table 'r' values. So hypothesis was rejected in these cases of boys and girls of Government School.

Table 42

To correlate Sense of humour and Memory of Government School boys

Variables	No	Mean	S.D	'r'	't'	L.S
Sense of humour Vs	50	2.96	0.9	0.0144	0.09	N.S
Memory	50	5.96	1.33			

Table-43

To correlate Sense of Humour and Memory of Government School Girls

Variables	No	Mean	S.D	'r'	't'	L.S
Sense of humour Vs	50	3.18	0.8	0.317	2.31	0.05
Memory	50	5.81	0.82			

The tables 42 and 43 shows that when sense of humour was correlated with memory the calculated 'r' values were greater than that of table 'r' values. Hence the hypothesis was accepted and proved that sense of humour and memory were interrelated in the case of Government School girls. When the sense of humour were related with memory it was found not to be significant in the case of boys of Government School.

Hypothesis-10

Different factors of Social Intelligence are related to each other in the case of Government Aided School.

Table 44

To correlate Patience with that of Co-operativeness, Confidence, Sensitivity, Recognition of Social Environment, Tactfulness, sense of Humour and Memory of Government Aided School Boys

Variables	No	Mean	S.D	'r'	't'	L.S
Patience Vs	50	17.74	2.7	0.4019	3.04	0.01
Cooperativeness	50	24.54	2.8			
Patience Vs	50	17.74	2.7	0.298	2.16	0.05
Confidence	50	18.64	2.94			

Patience Vs	50	17.74	2.7	0.3607	2.67	0.01
Sensitivity	50	19.48	2.22			
Patience Vs	50	17.74	2.7	0.129	0.90	N.S
Recognition of Social Environment	50	1.06	0.7			
Patience Vs	50	17.74	2.7	0.283	2.04	0.01
Tactfulness	50	3.46	1.09			
Patience Vs	50	17.74	2.7	0.136	0.95	N.S
Sense of Humour	50	3.24	1.17			
Patience Vs	50	17.74	2.7	0.147	1.02	N.S
Memory	50	6.62	1.44			

Table 45

To correlate Patience with that of Co-operativeness, Confidence, Sensitivity, Recognition of Social Environment, Tactfulness, sense of Humour and Memory of Government Aided School Girls

Variables	No	Mean	S.D	'r'	't'	L.S
Patience Vs	50	19.98	2.645	0.326	2.38	0.05
Cooperativeness	50	26.46	3.55			
Patience Vs	50	19.98	2.645	0.262	1.88	N.S
Confidence	50	20.08	2.2			
Patience Vs	50	19.98	2.645	0.63	5.62	0.01
Sensitivity	50	20.66	2.84			
Patience Vs	50	19.98	2.645			
Recognition of Social Environment	50	0.64	0.7	0.192	1.35	N.S
Patience Vs	50	19.98	2.645	0.011	0.07	N.S
Tactfulness	50	3.38	1.12			
Patience Vs	50	19.98	2.645	0.11	0.76	N.S
Sense of Humour	50	3.16	1.03			
Patience Vs	50	19.98	2.645	0.168	1.18	N.S
Memory	50	8.54	1.71			

From the tables 44 to 57 shows the correlation values among different factors of social intelligence in the case of Government Aided School. Tables 44 and 45 when patience was correlated with co-operativeness and sensitivity the calculated 'r' values greater than that of the table 'r' values . So hypothesis was accepted and proved that patients were interrelated with cooperativeness and sensitivity in the case of Government Aided School boys and girls. When the patience was related with confidence it was found to be significant in Government Aided School boys, where as other factors were correlated with patience it was not found to be significant in the case of Government Aided Schools boys and girls.

Table 46

To correlate Co-operativeness with that of Confidence, Sensitivity, Recognition of Social Environment, Tactfulness, Sense of humour and Memory of Government Aided School Boys

Variables	No	Mean	S.D	'r'	't'	L.S
Cooperativeness Vs	50	24.54	2.8	0.5828	4.96	0.01
Confidence	50	18.64	2.94			
Cooperativeness Vs	50	24.54	2.8	0.278	2.00	0.05
Sensitivity	50	19.48	2.22			
Cooperativeness Vs	50	24.54	2.8	0.17	1.19	N.S
Recognition of Social Environment	50	1.06	0.7			
Cooperativeness Vs	50	24.54	2.8	0.177	1.24	N.S
Tactfulness	50	3.46	1.09			
Cooperativeness Vs	50	24.54	2.8	0.214	1.51	N.S
Sense of Humour	50	3.24	1.17			
Cooperativeness Vs	50	24.54	2.8	0.264	1.89	N.S
Memory	50	6.62	1.44			

Table 47

To correlate Co-operativeness with that of Confidence, Sensitivity, Recognition of Social Environment, Tactfulness, Sense of humour and Memory of Government Aided School Girls

Variables	No	Mean	S.D	'r'	't'	L.S
Cooperativeness Vs	50	26.46	3.55	0.279	2.01	0.05
Confidence	50	20.08	2.2			
Cooperativeness Vs	50	26.46	3.55	0.246	1.75	N.S
Sensitivity	50	20.66	2.84			
Cooperativeness Vs	50	26.46	3.55			
Recognition of Social Environment	50	3.38	0.7	0.175	1.23	N.S
Cooperativeness Vs	50	26.46	3.55	0.0599	0.41	N.S
Tactfulness	50	3.38	1.12			

Cooperativeness Vs	50	26.46	3.55	0.086	0.59	N.S
Sense of Humour	50	3.16	1.03			
Cooperativeness Vs	50	26.46	3.55	0.061	0.35	N.S
Memory	50	8.54	1.71			

The tables 46 and 47 shows that co-operativeness was correlated with confidence, the calculated 'r' values were greater than that of table 'r' values. So hypothesis was accepted and proved that cooperativeness and confidence were interrelated in the case of Government Aided School boys and girls. When the cooperativeness was related with sensitivity, it was found to be significant in Government Aided School boys. Whereas, other factors were correlated with cooperativeness it was not found to be significant in the case of boys & girls of Government Aided School.

Table 48

To correlate Confidence with that of Sensitivity, Recognition of Social Environment, Tactfulness, Sense of humour and Memory of Government School Aided school boys

Variables	No	Mean	S.D	'r'	't'	L.S
Confidence Vs	50	18.64	2.94	0.288	2.08	0.05
Sensitivity	50	19.48	2.22			
Confidence Vs	50	18.64	2.94	0.184	1.29	N.S
Recognition of Social Environment	50	1.06	0.7			
Confidence Vs	50	18.64	2.94	0.166	1.16	N.S
Tactfulness	50	3.46	1.09			
Confidence Vs	50	18.64	2.94	0.161	1.13	N.S
Sense of Humour	50	3.24	1.17			
Confidence Vs	50	18.64	2.94	0.066	0.45	N.S
Memory	50	6.62	1.44			

The tables 48 and 49 shows that the confidence and correlated with sensitivity, the calculated 'r' values were greater than table 'r' values. So hypothesis was accepted and proved that confidence and sensitivity were interrelated in the case Government Aided School boys and girls. When the confidence was related with sense of humour it was found to be significant in Government Aided

School girls, where as other factors correlate with confidence it was found not to be significant in the case of boys and girls of Government Aided School.

Table 49

To correlate Confidence with that of Sensitivity, Recognition of Social Environment, Tactfulness, Sense of Humour and Memory of Government Aided School Girls

Variables	No	Mean	S.D	'r'	't'	L.S
Confidence Vs	50	20.08	2.2	0.337	2.47	0.05
Sensitivity50	20.66	2.84				
Confidence Vs	50	20.08	2.2	0.196	1.38	N.S
Recognition of Social Environment	50	0.64	0.7			
Confidence Vs	50	20.08	2.2	0.053	0.36	N.S
Tactfulness	50	3.38	1.12			
Confidence Vs	50	20.08	2.2	0.271	2.02	0.05
Sense of Humour	50	3.16	1.03			
Confidence Vs	50	20.08	2.2			
Memory	50	8.54	1.71	0.177	1.24	N.S

Table 50

To correlate Sensitivity with that of Recognition of Social Environment, Tactfulness, Sense of humour and Memory of Government Aided School boys

Variables	No	Mean	S.D	'r'	't'	L.S
Sensitivity Vs	50	19.48	2.22	0.134	0.93	N.S
Recognition of Social Environment	50	1.06	0.7			
Sensitivity Vs	50	19.48	2.22	0.024	0.16	N.S
Tactfulness	50	3.46	1.09			
Sensitivity Vs	50	19.48	2.22	0.072	0.50	N.S
Sense of Humour	50	3.24	1.17			
Sensitivity Vs	50	19.48	2.22	0.172	1.20	N.S
Memory	50	6.62	1.44			

The tables 50 and 51 shows that when sensitivity was correlated with various factors of social intelligence, the calculated 'r values were less than that of table 'r' values. So hypothesis was rejected in the case of boys and girls of Government Aided School.

Table 51

To correlate Sensitivity with that of Recognition of Social Environment, Tactfulness, Sense of humour and Memory of Government Aided School Girls

Variables	No	Mean	S.D	'r'	't'	L.S
Sensitivity Vs	50	20.66	2.84			
Recognition of Social Environment	50	0.64	0.7	0.139	0.97	N.S
Sensitivity Vs	50	20.66	2.84	0.086	0.59	N.S
Tactfulness	50	3.38	1.12			
Sensitivity Vs	50	20.66	2.84	0.081	0.56	N.S
Sense of Humour	50	3.16	1.03			
Sensitivity Vs	50	20.66	2.84	0.176	1.23	N.S
Memory	50	8.54	1.71			

The tables 50 and 51 shows that when sensitivity was correlated with various factors of social intelligence, the calculated 'r values were less than that of table 'r' values. So hypothesis was rejected in the case of boys and girls of Government Aided School.

Table 52

To correlate Recognition of Social Environment with tactfulness, Sense of humour and Memory of Government Aided School Boys

Variables	No	Mean	S.D	'r'	't'	L.S
Recognition of Social Environment Vs	50	1.06	0.7	0.088	0.61	N.S
Tactfulness	50	3.46	1.09			
Recognition of Social Environment Vs	50	1.06	0.7	0.066	0.45	N.S
Sense of Humour	50	3.24	1.17			
Recognition of Social Environment Vs	50	1.06	0.7	0.142	0.99	N.S
Memory	50	6.62	1.44			

The tables 52 and 53 shows that when recognition of social environment and correlated with tactfulness and sense of humour the calculated 'r' values were greater than table 'r' values. So hypothesis was accepted and proved that recognition of social environment were interrelated with tactfulness and sense of humour in the case of Government Aided School girls. Whereas other factors were correlated with recognition of social environment it was not found to be significant in the case of boys and girls of Government Aided School.

Table 53

To correlate Recognition of Social Environment with tactfulness, Sense of humour and Memory of Government Aided School girls

Variables	No	Mean	S.D	'r'	't'	L.S
Recognition of Social Environment Vs	50	0.64	0.7	0.370	2.75	0.01
Tactfulness	50	3.38	1.12			
Recognition of Social Environment Vs	50	0.64	0.7	0.377	2.81	0.01
Sense of Humour	50	3.16	1.03			
Recognition of Social Environment Vs	50	0.64	0.7	0.041	0.28	N.S
Memory	50	8.54	1.71			

TABLE 54

To correlate Tactfulness with Sense of humour and Memory of Government Aided School Boys

Variables	No	Mean	S.D	'r'	't'	L.S
Tactfulness Vs	50	3.46	1.09	0.279	2.01	0.05
Sense of Humour	50	3.24	1.17			
Tactfulness Vs	50	3.46	1.09	0.197	1.26	N.S
Memory	50	6.62	1.44			

Table 55

To correlate Tactfulness with Sense of humour and Memory of Government Aided School Girls

Variables	No	Mean	S.D	'r'	't'	L.S
Tactfulness Vs	50	3.38	1.12	0.139	0.97	N.S
Sense of Humour	50	3.16	1.03			
Tactfulness Vs	50	3.38	1.12	0.24	1.71	N.S
Memory	50	8.54	1.71			

The tables 54 and 55 shows that when the tactfulness and correlated with sense of humour, the calculated 'r' values were greater than table 'r' values. So hypothesis was accepted and proved that tactfulness and sense of humour were interrelated in the case of Government Aided School boys. Whereas other factors correlated with tactfulness it was found not to be significant in the case of boys and girls of Government Aided School.

Table 56

To correlate Sense of humour and Memory of Government Aided School Boys

Variables	No	Mean	S.D	'r'	't'	L.S
Sense of humour Vs	50	3.24	1.17	0.309	2.2	0.05
Memory	50	6.62	1.44			

Table 57

To correlate Sense of humour and Memory of Government Aided School Girls

Variables	No	Mean	S.D	'r'	't'	L.S
Sense of humour Vs	50	3.16	1.03	2.71	1.95	N.S
Memory	50	8.54	1.710.82			

The tables 56 and 57 shows that when the sense of humour correlated with memory, the calculated 'r' values were greater than table 'r' values. In the case of Government Aided School boys. Hence the hypothesis was accepted and proved that sense of humour and memory were interrelated. Where as in the case of Government Aided School girls, the calculated 'r' values were less than that of table 'r' values. So the hypothesis was rejected in this case.

Hypothesis-11

Various factors of social intelligence are interrelated among themselves of Private School.

From the tables 58 to 71 shows the correlation values among different factors of social intelligence in the case of Private School. Tables 58 and 59 show that when patience was correlated with cooperativeness the calculated 'r' value were greater than table 'r'

Table 58

To correlate Patience with that of Co-operatives, Confidence, Sensitivity, Recognition of Social Environment, Tactfulness, sense of Humour and Memory of Private School Boys

Variables	No	Mean	S.D	'r'	't'	L.S
Patience Vs	50	18.274	3.516	0.474	3.72	0.01
Cooperativeness	50	25.215	3.46			
Patience Vs	50	18.274	3.516	0.474	3.72	0.01
Confidence	50	18.901	2.5			
Patience Vs	50	18.274	3.516	0.13	0.90	N.S
Sensitivity	50	20.529	2.6			
Patience Vs	50	18.274	3.516	0.079	0.54	N.S
Recognition of Social Environment	50	0.843	0.7			
Patience Vs	50	18.274	3.516	0.181	0.98	N.S
Tactfulness	50	3.627	0.87			
Patience Vs	50	18.274	3.516	0.121	0.84	N.S
Sense of Humour	50	3.549	1.269			
Patience Vs	50	18.274	3.516	0.15	1.05	N.S
Memory 50	8.372	2.16				

Table 59

To correlate Patience with that of Co-operativeness, Confidence, Sensitivity, Recognition of Social Environment, Tactfulness, sense of Humour and Memory of Private School Girls

Variables	No	Mean	S.D	'r'	't'	L.S
Patience Vs	50	20.5	2.10	0.588	5.03	0.01
Cooperativeness	50	26.58	2.81			
Patience Vs	50	20.5	2.10	0.129	0.90	N.S
Confidence	50	20.62	1.75			
Patience Vs	50	20.5	2.10	0.488	3.87	0.01
Sensitivity	50	21.26	2.04			
Patience Vs	50	20.5	2.10	0.046	0.31	N.S
Recognition of Social Environment	50	0.62	0.7			
Patience Vs	50	20.5	2.10	0.133	0.24	N.S
Tactfulness	50	4.28	1.08			
Patience Vs	50	20.5	2.10	0.164	1.48	N.S
Sense of Humour	50	3.68	1.7			
Patience Vs	50	20.5	2.10	0.221	0.52	N.S
Memory	50	8.92	0.16			

values. So hypothesis was accepted and proved that patience and co-operativeness were, interrelated in the case of boys and girls of Private School. When the patience was related with confidence, it was found to be significant in Private School boys, when the patience was related with sensitivity it was found to be significant in Private School Girls, were as other factor were correlated with patience it was found not to be significant in the case of Private School boys and girls.

Table 60

To correlate Co-operativeness with that of Confidence, Sensitivity, Recognition of Social Environment, Tactfulness, Sense of humour and Memory of Private School Boys

Variables	No	Mean	S.D	'r'	't'	L.S
Cooperativeness Vs	50	25.215	3.46	0.320	2.33	0.05
Confidence	50	18.901	2.5			
Cooperativeness Vs	50	25.215	3.46	0.011	0.07	N.S
Sensitivity	50	20.529	2.6			
Cooperativeness Vs	50	25.215	3.46	0.083	0.57	N.S
Recognition of Social Environment	50	0.843	0.7			
Cooperativeness Vs	50	25.215	3.46	0.142	0.99	N.S
Tactfulness	50	3.627	0.87			
Cooperativeness Vs	50	25.215	3.46	0.180	1.26	N.S
Sense of Humour	50	3.549	1.269			
Cooperativeness Vs	50	25.215	3.46	0.33	2.42	0.05
Memory	50	8.372	2.16			

The tables 60 and 61 shows that co-operativeness was correlated with confidence, the calculated 'r' values were greater than that of table 'r' values. So hypothesis was accepted and proved that cooperativeness and confidence were interrelated in the case of Private School boys and girls. When the co-operativeness was related with sense of humour it was found to be significant in Private School girls, when the cooperativeness was related with memory it was found to be significant in Private School boys. Whereas, other factors were correlated with cooperativeness it was not found to be significant in the case of Private School boys and girls.

Table 61

To correlate Co-operativeness with that of Confidence, Sensitivity, Recognition of Social Environment, Tactfulness, Sense of humour and Memory of Private School Girls

Variables	No	Mean	S.D	'r'	't'	L.S
Cooperativeness Vs	50	26.58	2.81	-0.325	2.38	0.05
Confidence	50	20.62	1.75			
Cooperativeness Vs	50	26.58	2.81	0.482	0.87	N.S
Sensitivity	50	21.26	2.04			
Cooperativeness Vs	50	26.58	2.81	0.1997	1.42	N.S
Recognition of Social Environment	50	0.62	0.7			
Cooperativeness Vs	50	26.58	2.81	0.0857	0.59	N.S
Tactfulness	50	4.28	1.08			
Cooperativeness Vs	50	26.58	2.81	0.4258	3.26	0.01
Sense of Humour	50	3.68	1.7			
Cooperativeness Vs	50	26.58	2.81	0.0109	0.07	N.S
Memory	50	8.92	0.16			

The tables 62 and 63 shows that when confidence was correlated with memory the calculated 'r' values were greater than that of table 'r' values. So hypothesis was accepted and proved that confidence and memory were interrelated in the case of Private School boys. Whereas other factors were correlated with confidence it was found not to be significant in the case of Private School boys and girls.

Table 62

To correlate Confidence with that of Sensitivity, Recognition of Social Environment, Tactfulness, Sense of humour and Memory of Private School boys

Variables	No	Mean	S.D	'r'	't'	L.S
Confidence Vs	50	18.901	2.5	0.036	0.24	N.S
Sensitivity	50	20.529	2.6			
Confidence Vs	50	18.901	2.5	0.031	0.21	N.S
Recognition of Social Environment	50	0.843	0.7			
Confidence Vs	50	18.901	2.5	0.134	0.93	N.S
Tactfulness	50	3.627	0.87			
Confidence Vs	50	18.901	2.5	0.267	1.91	N.S
Sense of Humour	50	3.549	1.269			
Confidence Vs	50	18.901	2.5	0.366	2.72	0.01
Memory	50	8.372	2.16			

Table 63

To correlate Confidence with that of Sensitivity, Recognition of Social Environment, Tactfulness, Sense of Humour and Memory of Private School Girls

Variables	No	Mean	S.D	'r'	't'	L.S
Confidence Vs	50	20.62	1.75	0.081	0.56	N.S
Sensitivity	50	21.26	2.04			
Confidence Vs	50	20.62	1.75	0.003	0.02	N.S
Recognition of Social Environment	50	0.62	0.7			
Confidence Vs	50	20.62	1.75	0.124	0.86	N.S
Tactfulness	50	4.28	1.08			
Confidence Vs	50	20.62	1.75	0.0809	0.56	N.S
Sense of Humour	50	3.68	1.7			
Confidence Vs	50	20.62	1.75	0.1518	1.06	N.S
Memory	50	8.92	0.16			

Table 64

To correlate Sensitivity with that of Recognition of Social Environment, Tactfulness, Sense of humour and Memory of Private School boys

Variables	No	Mean	S.D	'r'	't'	L.S
Sensitivity Vs	50	20.529	2.6	0.060	0.41	N.S
Recognition of Social Environment	50	0.843	0.7			
Sensitivity Vs	50	20.529	2.6	0.0456	0.31	N.S
Tactfulness	50	3.627	0.87			
Sensitivity Vs	50	20.529	2.6	0.155	1.08	N.S
Sense of Humour	50	3.549	1.269			
Sensitivity Vs	50	20.529	2.6	0.222	1.57	N.S
Memory	50	8.372	2.16			

The tables 64 and 65 shows that when sensitivity was correlated with tactfulness and sense of humour, the calculated r values were greater than that of table 'r' values. So hypothesis was accepted and proved the sensitivity were interrelated with tactfulness and sense of humour in the case of Private School girls. Whereas other factors were correlated with sensitivity, it was found not to be significant in the case of boys and girls of Private School.

Table 65

To correlate Sensitivity with that of Recognition of Social Environment, Tactfulness, Sense of humour and Memory of Private School Girls

Variables	No	Mean	S.D	'r'	't'	L.S
Sensitivity Vs	50	21.26	2.04	0.007	0.04	N.S
Recognition of Social Environment	50	0.62	0.7			
Sensitivity Vs	50	21.26	2.04	0.368	2.74	0.01
Tactfulness	50	4.28	1.08			
Sensitivity Vs	50	21.26	2.04	0.35	2.58	0.01
Sense of Humour	50	3.68	1.7			
Sensitivity Vs	50	21.26	2.04	0.043	0.29	N.S
Memory	50	8.92	0.16			

Table 66

To correlate Recognition of Social Environment with tactfulness, Sense of humour and Memory of Private School boys

Variables	No	Mean	S.D	'r'	't'	L.S
Recognition of Social Environment Vs	50	0.843	0.7	0.194	1.37	N.S
Tactfulness	50	3.627	0.87			
Recognition of Social Environment Vs	50	0.843	0.7	0.0074	0.05	N.S
Sense of Humour	50	3.549	1.269			
Recognition of Social Environment Vs	50	0.843	0.7	0.159	1.11	N.S
Memory	50	8.372	2.16			

The tables 66 and 67 shows that when recognition of social environment was correlated with sense of humour, tactfulness and memory the calculated 'r' values were less than that of table 'r' values. So hypothesis was rejected in these cases of boys and girls of Private School.

Table 67

To correlate Recognition of Social Environment with tactfulness, Sense of humour and Memory of Private School girls

Variables	No	Mean	S.D	'r'	't'	L.S
Recognition of Social N.SEnvironment Vs		50	0.62	0.7	0.25	0.17
Tactfulness	50	4.28	1.08			
Recognition of Social Environment Vs	50	0.62	0.7	0.001	0.006	N.S
Sense of Humour	50	3.68	1.7			
Recognition of Social Environment Vs	50	0.62	0.7	0.079	0.54	N.S
Memory	50	8.92	0.16			

Table 68

To correlate Tactfulness with Sense of humour and Memory of Private School boys

Variables	No	Mean	S.D	'r'	't'	L.S
Tactfulness Vs	50	3.627	0.87			
Sense of Humour	50	3.549	1.269	0.8	9.23	0.01
Tactfulness Vs	50	3.627	0.87			
Memory	50	8.372	2.16	0.318	2.32	0.05

Table 69

To correlate Tactfulness with Sense of humour and Memory of Private School Girls

Variables	No	Mean	S.D	'r'	't'	L.S
Tactfulness Vs	50	4.28	1.08			
Sense of Humour	50	3.68	1.7	0.268	1.92	N.S
Tactfulness Vs	50	4.28	1.08			
Memory	50	8.92	0.16	0.0188	0.13	N.S

The tables 68 and 69 shows that when tactfulness was correlated with sense of humour and memory the calculated 'r' values were greater than that of table 'r' values. So hypothesis was accepted and proved that tactfulness were interrelated with sense of humour, and memory in the case of Private School boys. Whereas other factor was correlated with tactfulness it was found not to be significant in the case of Private School girls.

Table 70

To correlate Sense of humour with that of Memory of Private School boys

Variables	No	Mean	S.D	'r'	't'	L.S
Sense of humour Vs	50	3.549	1.269	0.141	0.98	N.S
Memory	50	8.372	2.16			

Table 71

To correlate Sense of humour with that of Memory of Private School Girls

Variables	No	Mean	S.D	'r'	't'	L.S
Sense of humour Vs	50	3.68	1.7	0.344	2.53	0.01
Memory	50	8.92	0.16			

The tables 70 and 71 shows that when sense of humour was correlated with memory the calculated 'r' values were greater than that of table 'r' values. Hence the hypothesis was accepted and proved that sense of humour and memory were interrelated in the case of Private School girls. When the sense of humour were related with memory it was found not to be significant in the case of boys of Private School.

Conclusion

Statistical techniques used in this chapter analyzed the data comparing the social intelligence & life satisfaction of 300 students from government, government aided and Private School in the Tuticorin District based on the results obtained, hypothesis framed were either approved or disapproved. The succeeding chapter explains the brief summary about the present study.

5

Summary, Findings and Conclusion

Introduction

The present study aims at bringing to highlight how far we have proceeded the work sincerely in the subject of social intelligence and life satisfaction among XI standard students. This chapter furnishes a short description of all the preceding chapters, highlights the main findings of the study and point out some implications and recommendations for application of the findings.

Sample

Total 300 students were taken for the study of which 100 from Government School, 100 from Government Aided School and 100 from Private Schools in each category it contains 50 boys and 50 girls. All the students chosen for the study were studying in XI standard in Tuticorin District.

Statement of the Problem

Social intelligence and life satisfaction among higher secondary school students was chosen as the topic for the present study.

Government School, Government Aided School and Private Schools were selected to conduct the study. Data were collected from 300 students (150 boys and 150 girls). In order to test the hypothesis proposed, the investigator statistically analyzed the data.

Objectives

1. To relate life satisfaction with that of social intelligence.
2. To find out the relationship between social intelligence with that of educational status of the parent in the case of total sample.
3. To identify associations existing between educational status of the parents and life satisfaction of the total sample.
4. To recognize the impact of type of family on social intelligence and life satisfaction of the total sample.
5. To know the impact of Gender on type of school, social intelligence, life satisfaction and various factors of social intelligence.
6. To interrelate various factors of social intelligence in the case of Government School, Government Aided School and Private School students.

FINDINGS AND DISCUSSIONS

Hypothesis I

Life satisfaction scores of the students will modify social intelligence.

The hypothesis was accepted and proved that life satisfaction scores modified the level of social intelligence of boys and girls of Private School and the boys of Government School. Where as in the case of boys and girls of Government Aided School and girls of Government School it was not found to be significant hence the hypothesis was rejected in these cases.

Hypothesis II

Social intelligence has no impact on education status of the students.

The hypothesis was accepted and proved that intelligence had no impact education status of the students in the case of boys and girls from Government School, Government Aided School and Private School.

Hypothesis III

Social intelligence does not depend on the type of family.

The hypothesis was accepted and proved that intelligence did not depend upon the type of family of the students in the case of boys and girls from Government School, Government Aided School and Private Schools.

Hypothesis IV

Life satisfaction does not depend on Education status.

The hypothesis was accepted and proved that life satisfaction did not depend on education status of the students in the case of boys and girls from Private School, Government School and girls from Government Aided School. Where as in the case of boys of Government Aided School. It was found to be significant. Hence hypothesis was rejected in this case.

Hypothesis V

Life satisfaction has no impact with the type of family.

The hypothesis was accepted and proved that life satisfaction had no impact with the type of family of the students in the case of boys and girls from Government School, Government Aided School and Private School.

Hypothesis VI

Gender plays an important role on life satisfaction of students.

The hypothesis was accepted and proved that gender played an important role on life satisfaction of student in the case of Private School and Government Aided School. Where as in the case of Government School. It was not found to be significant. Hence the hypothesis was rejected in this case.

Hypothesis VII

Gender plays an important role on total score of social intelligence.

The hypothesis was accepted and proved that gender played an important role on total score of social intelligence of student in the case of Private School and Government Aided School. Where as in the case of Government School. It was not found to be significant. Hence the hypothesis was rejected in this case.

Hypothesis VIII

Gender plays very important role on various factors of social intelligence of the total sample.

The hypothesis was accepted and proved that gender played very important role on patience factors or social intelligence in the case of boys and girls of Private School and Government Aided School. Where as in the case of Government School. It was not found to be significant. Hence the hypothesis was rejected in this case.

The hypothesis was accepted and proved that gender played an important role on co-operativeness factors of social intelligence in the case of boys and girls of Private Schools. Where as in the case of boys and girls of Government Aided School and Government School, it was not found to be significant. Hence the hypothesis was rejected in these cases.

The hypothesis was accepted and proved that gender played very important role on confidence factors of social intelligence in the case of boys and girls of Private Schools, Government Aided School and Government School.

The hypothesis was rejected and proved that gender did not play important role on sensitivity factors of social intelligence in the case of Private Schools, Government Aided School and Government School.

The hypothesis was accepted and proved that gender played very important role on recognition of social environment factors of social intelligence in the case boys and girls of Government Aided School. Where as in the case of Private Schools and Government School. It was not found to be significant. Hence the hypothesis was rejected in these cases.

The hypothesis was accepted and proved that gender played very important role on tactfulness in the case boys and girls of Government School and Private School. Where as in the case of boys and girls of Government Aided School. It was not found to be significant. Hence the hypothesis was rejected in this case.

The hypothesis was accepted and proved that gender played very important role on sense of humour factors of social intelligence in the case of boys and girls of Private School. Where as in the case of Government Aided School and Government School. It was not found to be significant. Hence the hypothesis was rejected in these cases.

The hypothesis was accepted and proved that gender played very important role on memory factors of social intelligence in the case boys and girls of Government Aided School. Where as in the case of Private Schools and Government School. It was not found to be significant. Hence the hypothesis was rejected in these cases.

Hypothesis IX

Various factors of social intelligence are rejected to each other of Government School.

The hypothesis was accepted and proved that patience and confidence where, interrelated in the case boys and girls of Government School. When patience was related with co-operativeness and sensitivity it was found to be significant in Government School girls, where as other factor where correlated with patience it was not found to be significant in the case of boys and girls of Government School. Hence the hypothesis was rejected in this case.

The hypothesis was accepted and proved that co-operativeness was related with confidence and sensitivity in the case of boys and girls of Government School. When the co-operativeness was related with recognition of school environment and tactfulness it was found to be significant in boys or Government School. Whereas other factors were correlated with co-operativeness it was not found to be significant in the case of boys and girls of Government School. Hence the hypothesis was rejected in this case.

The hypothesis was rejected and proved that confidence and various factors of social intelligence where not related in the case of Government School boys and girls.

The hypothesis was accepted and proved that the sensitivity and sense of humour where inter related in the case of Government School girls. When the sensitivity were related with other factors it was found not to be significant in the case of boys and girls of Government School. Hence the hypothesis was rejected in this case.

The hypothesis was rejected when the recognition of social environment was correlated with sense of humour, tactfulness and memory. It was not found to be significant in the case of boys and girls of Government School.

The hypothesis was rejected when tactfulness was correlated with sense of humour and memory. It was not found to be significant in the case of boys and girls of Government School.

The hypothesis was accepted and proved that sense of humour and memory where interrelated in the case of Government School girls. When the sense of humour where related with memory it was not found to be significant in the case of Government School boys. Hence the hypothesis was rejected in this case.

Hypothesis X

Different factors of social intelligence are related to each other in the case of Government Aided School.

The hypothesis was accepted and proved that patients were interrelated with co-operativeness and sensitivity in the case of Government Aided School girls and boys. When the patience was related with confidence it was found to be significant in

Government Aided School boys. Whereas other factors were correlated with patience it was found not to be significant in the case of Government Aided School boys and girls. Hence hypothesis was rejected in these cases.

The hypothesis was accepted and proved that co-operativeness and confidence were interrelated in the case of Government Aided School boys and girls. When the co-operativeness was related with sensitivity it was found to be significant in Government Aided School boys. Whereas other factors were correlated with co-operativeness it was not found to be significant in the case of boys and girls of Government Aided School. Hence the hypothesis was rejected in these cases.

The hypothesis was accepted and proved that confidence and sensitivity were interrelated in the case of Government Aided School boys and girls. When the confidence was related with sense of humour it was found to be significant in Government Aided School girls, where as other factors were correlate with confidence it was not found to be significant in the case of boys and girls of Government Aided School. Hence the hypothesis was rejected in these cases.

The hypothesis was rejected and proved that sensitivity and various factors of social intelligence are not interrelated in the case of boys and girls of Government Aided School.

The hypothesis was accepted and proved that recognition of social environment were interrelated with tactfulness and sense of humour in the case of Government Aided School girls. Whereas other factors were correlated with recognition of social environment it was not found to be significant in the case of boys and girls of Government Aided School. Hence the hypothesis was rejected in this case.

The hypothesis was accepted and proved that tactfulness and sense of humour were interrelated in the case of Government Aided School boys. Whereas other factors correlated with tactfulness it was not found to be significant in the case of boys and girls of Government Aided School. Hence the hypothesis was rejected in this case.

The hypothesis was accepted and proved that sense of humour and memory were interrelated. Where as in the case of Government Aided School girls. It was found not to be significant. Hence the hypothesis was rejected in this case.

Hypothesis XI

Various factors of social intelligence are interrelated among themselves of private school.

The hypothesis was accepted and proved that patience and co-operativeness were interrelated in the case of boys and girls of Private School . When the patience was related with confidence it was found to be significant in Private School boys. When the patience was related with sensitivity it was found to be significant in Private School girls, where as other factors were correlated with patience it was not found to be significant in the case of Private School boys and girls. Hence the hypothesis was rejected in these cases.

The hypothesis was proved that co-operativeness and confidence was interrelated in the case of Private School boys and girls. When the co-operativeness was related with sense of humour it was not found to be significant in Private School girls, when the co-operativeness was related with memory it was found to be significant in Private School boys. Whereas other factors were correlated with co-operativeness it was not found to be significant in the case of Private School boys and girls. Hence the hypothesis was rejected in this case.

The hypothesis was accepted and proved that confidence and memory were interrelated in the case of Private School boys. Whereas other factors were correlated with confidence it was not found to be significant in the case of Private School boys and girls. Hence the hypothesis was rejected in these cases.

The hypothesis was accepted and proved that sensitivity were interrelated with tactfulness and sense of humour in the case of Private School girls. Whereas other factors were correlated with sensitivity it was not found to be significant in the case of boys and girls of Private School. Hence the hypothesis was rejected in these cases.

The hypothesis was rejected when recognition of social environment was correlated with sense of humour, tactfulness and memory it was found not to be significant in the case of boys and girls of Private School.

The hypothesis was accepted and proved that tactfulness were interrelated with sense of humour, and memory in the case of Private School boys. Whereas other factors was correlated with tactfulness it was not found not to be significant in the case of Private School girls. Hence the hypothesis was rejected in this case.

The hypothesis was accepted and proved that sense of humour and memory were interrelated in the case of Private School girls. When the sense of humour were related with memory it was not found to be significant in the case of boys of private school.

Educational Implications

The finding of the present investigation are important for the improvement in the quality of Education. The following are some of the major recommendation to implicate the Life satisfaction and social intelligence of the students.

1. Educators and administrators should bring about an awareness among students to give more importance to develop Life satisfaction and social intelligence.
2. Parents role is necessary to develop Life satisfaction of students through guiding, directing, stimulating and encouraging.
3. Lectures should provide inspiring leadership in developing Life satisfaction and social intelligence among students.
4. Emotional development programmes and seminar are to be arranged in the classrooms.
5. Early identification and environmental stimulation by teacher are very much essential. They should conduct Life satisfaction and social intelligence tests in the classrooms.

Emmons (1986) found that positive affect is related to the Degree to which one accomplishes their goals, negative affect is related to the individual's ambivalence about their goals and Conflict between their goals, and life satisfaction was highest for those who had goals that were very important to them. Cantor (1994) believes that an individual's goals are Determined by one's life circumstances, expectations of the Culture, and the person's idiosyncratic needs. People can Accomplish their goals in a variety of ways, but those with high Life satisfaction have developed effective strategies for meeting their Needs within the constraints of cultural expectations and life Circumstances. Intrinsic goals reflect Inherent growth tendencies and satisfy inherent psychological Needs whereas extrinsic goals are imposed on the individual by Society and are sought for the approval of others or some other End. Specially, the extrinsic goals of desire for material.

Suggestions for Further Research

1. Social intelligence and academic achievement among the secondary school students.
2. Social intelligence in relation to creativity among higher secondary school students.
3. Life satisfaction and intellectual ability among the high school students.
4. Life satisfaction, intelligence and learning process among the higher secondary school students.
5. Life satisfaction and self confidence among the secondary school students.

Bibliography

1. **Bailey and Miller (1998)**, Predicting Life Satisfaction, Personality and Social Psychology Bulletin, in August Edition.
2. **Binet, A. (1916), The Development of Intelligence in Children** (translated by E.S. Kite). Vineland. N.J.: Training School.

3. **Cacioppo, J. T., & Petty, R. E. (1982),** The need for cognition. Journal of Personality and Social Psychology, 42, 116-131.
4. **Campbell A., et. al (1976),** The quality of American life New York: Rissell sage Foundation.
5. **Cattell, R.B. (1940),** Theory of Fluid and Crystalized intelligence: A Critical experiment, Journal of Educational Psychology, 31, 161-179.
6. **Chaplin, J.P (1965),** Dictionary of psychology.
7. **Chatterjee, A. and Dutta Roy. D (1991),** Awareness of external environment, environmental sati Applied Psychology, 29,2, 74-77.
8. **Chauhan, S.S. (1996),** Advanced Educational Psychology, Sixth Revised Edition, Delhi: Vikas Publishing House Pvt. Ltd.
9. **Cheung, C. (2000),** Studying as a source of life satisfaction among university students. College Student Journal, 34, 79-96.
10. **Cohen, A. R., et.al., (1955),** An experimental investigation of need for cognition. Journal of Abnormal and Social Psychology, 51, 291-294.
11. **Diener, E., and R., Larsen, R., (1985),** The Satisfaction with Life Scale. Journal of Personality Assessment 49, 71-75.
12. **Dockrell, W.B. (1974),** On Intelligence, London: Methuen.
13. **Dr. Bhatnagar A.B. (2004),** Educational Psychology, Meerut. Surya Publications.
14. **Dr. Mangal S.K. (1983),** Psychological Foundation of Education, Ludhiana: Rampracash Tandon.
15. **Dr. R.S. Sharma (2004),** Teaching of Social Science, by Surya Publicaitons.
16. **Dutta Roy, D. & Mukhopadhyay, S. (1999),** Organizational coping and organizational commitment across organizational hiearchies in heavy engineering organizations, Journal of Behavioural Sciences. 10, 2, 5-20.

17. **Dutta Roy, D. (2000)**, Maximizing coefficient alpha of state anxiety inventory in repeated measurement design, Indian Journal of Psychometry and Education, 31,2,111-114.

18. **Dutta Roy, D. and Mallik, R. (2000),** Ranking General aptitudes for success in computer programming, Journal of the Indian Academy of applied Psychology, Journal of the Indian Academy of Applied Psychology, 26, 1-2, 135-139.

19. **Dutta Roy, D.(1996),** Personality model of fine artists,Creativity Research Journal, 9,4,391-394.

20. **Dutta Roy, D. (1991),** A comparative study of organizational awareness strategies in private and public sector, Decision, 18,1,41-44.

21. **Dutta Roy, D. (2002),** Computer programming job analysis, Management and Labour Studies. 27,4,255-262.

22. **Dutta Roy, D.(1991),** A model of change in Organizational health to improve Quality of life, Social Science International, Vol.16, No.4, pp. 189-191.

23. **Esther N Goody (1995),** "Social Intelligence and Interaction" Published by Cambridge University.

24. **Fisher and Bradley. J (1995),** Successful Aging, Life Satisfaction and Generativity in Later Life, International Journal of Aging and Human – Development, Vol. 1, No. 3, pp. 239-50. ERIC.

25. **Guilford, J.P. (1967),** The Nature of Human Intelligence, New York: McGraw Hill.

26. **Guilford, J.P. Hopener, R. (1971),** The Analysis of Intelligence, New York, McGraw Hill.

27. **Harry Elmer Barnes (2004).** History and Social Intelligence , Kessenger.

28. **Hawkins** and **Barbara**, A Validity and Reliability of a Five Dimensional Life Satisfaction Index, Mental Retardation, Vol. 33, No. 5, p. 295-303, Oct. 1995.

29. **Henry – Caroln. S,** and **Lovelace Sandra. G. (1995),** Family Resources and Adolescent Family Life Satisfaciton in Remarried Family Households, Journal of Family Issues; Vol. 16, No. 6, pp. 765-86, Nov. 1995.

30. **Henry and Carolyn. S (1994)**, Family System Characteristics, Parental Behaviours and Adolescent Family Life Satisfaction, Family Relations, Vol. 43, No. 4, p. 447-55, Oct. 1994.

31. **Hoffman, R.E. (1987).** Computer simulations of neural information processing and the schizophrenia-mania dichotomy. Archives of General Psychiatry, 44:178-188.

32. **Huebner and Scott. E. (1994)**, Life Satisfaction Scale and the Piers – Harris Self-Concept Scale, Psychology in the School, Vol. 33, No. 31, p. 273-77, Oct. 1994.

33. **Humphreys, L.G. (1971),** Theory of Intelligence, In R. Cancro (Ed), Intelligence: Genertic and Environmental Influences (31-55), New York; Grune and Stratton.

34. **Hunt, T. (1928),** The measurement of Social Intelligence, Journal of Applied Psychology, 12, 317-334.

35. **Leone, C., & Dalton, C. (1988),** Some effects of the need for cognition on course grades. Perceptual and Motor Skills, 67, 175-178.

36. **Lewis, Virginia. G and Borders. L (1995),** Life Satisfaction of Single Middle-Aged Professional Women, Journal of Counselling and Development, Vol. 74, No. 1, p. 100, Sep. 1995.

37. **Mayer, J.D. and Salovey, P. (1993),** The intelligence of Emotional Intelligence; 433 - 422.

38. **Mc Clelland, B.C. (1973),** Testing for competence rather than Intelligence, American Psychologist, 28, 1-14.

39. **Meeker, M.N. (1969),** The structure of Intellect: its interpretation and uses, columbas, Ohio: Charles E. Merril.

40. **Park, Douglas et.al. (1994)**, The Influence of Separation Orientation on Life Satisfaction in the Elderly, International

Journal of Aging and Human – Development, Vol. 39, No. 2, p. 117-07, 1994.

41. **Piaget, J. (1947),** The Psychology of Intelligence, London: Routledge and Kegal Paul.

42. **Pintner, R. and Upshall, C.C. (1928),** Some results of social Intelligence Tests, School and Society, 27, 369-370.

43. **Spearman, C. (1923),** The Nature of "Intelligence" and the Principles of Cognition, London: McMillan.

44. **Spearman, C. (1923),** The Nature of "Intelligence" and the Principles of cognition, London: Mac Millan.

45. **Spearman, C. (1927),** The Abilities of Man, New York: Mac Millan.

46. **Stern, W. (1914),** The Psychological Methods of Testing Intelligence, (Translated by G.M. Whipple) Educational Psychology Monographs.

47. **Thorndike, E.L. (1927),** The Measurement of Intelligence, New York: \/Teachers College, Columbia University.

48. **Vernon, P.F. (1948),** Indices of Item consistency and validity, British Journal of Psychology 1, 152-166.

49. **Young and Margaret. H**, The Effect of Parental Supportive Behaviour on Life Satisfaction of Adolescent Offspring, Journal of Marriage and the Family, Vol. 57, No. 3, p. 813-22, Aug. 1995.

APPENDIX – I

Social Intelligence Scale

INSTRUCTIONS

In this booklet there are some statements regarding the way in which we behave, feel and act. We want your first response. Please try to make your best possible answer honestly and sincerely. Read and understand each question properly and then put your mark on any cell against every statement on the answer-sheet by making the sign of cross (X) please do not omit any question. Your answer will be kept strictly confidential. We need your full cooperation.

Please read the following statements carefully and among the three responses "given for each of them, pick up the one which seems to you to be the most likely way in which you would respond. You are to choose only one response from a, b and c and mark a cross (X) on the appropriate cell on the answer-sheet.

Sr. No.	STATEMENT	a	b	c
1.	Your servant has taken a days leave.	You are the first to volunteer help.	You will help if nobody else does.	You find some excuse and avoid helping.
2.	When you hear about a crime.	You sympathise you solely with the indifferent Victims.	You remain indifferent.	You do both, sympathies with the victims and emphathise with the criminals.
3.	You have been given an award for academic excellence.	How did manage it?	I deserved it?	Well, nobody else could have got it.
4.	You are forced to rewrite some of your notes because somebody stole them.	I will kill the person.	I wonder why somebody had to do this.	I will never forgive him / her.
5.	You are requested to switch off the music system as your neighbour is having a evere headache.	You immediately comply.	You ignore the request.	You grumble and argue.
6.	You come across an accident where a car collided with an elephant. The former was damaged and the latter died. What strikes you first?	The damaged car received.	The dead elephant.	Both.
7.	You are asked to join a rough trek.	I am determined to give it a try.	I wonder if 1 can stand the strain.	Oh! I won't risk it.
8.	Some one who is dependent on you spends your hard earned money on 'gambling.	You repirmand severly.	You talk it over.	You decide to throw him out.
9.	If you are asked to come for a picnic you do not really want to go for but know your friends would like you to.	You will go.	You refuse point blank.	You will try your best avoid going if it were possible
10.	You hear that some anti-social elements have been given capital punishment.	You are happy.	You are relieved.	You are against capital punishment.
11.	You are invited for a grand party.	I hope I know people there.	I guess I'll make friends.	I wish I did not have to go.
12.	You are asked to make a speech at public function.	Gosh I am nervous.	I will give them a talk to remember.	I wonder if a substitute can be found.
13.	You come out of a restaurant and find a beggar out side.	You give Kirn some money.	You ignore him.	You feel guilty.
14.	If you had to share your room with a distant cousin for a week.	You hesitate.	You refuse.	You agree immediately.
15.	At a group meeting you find it impossible to flut forward a very pertinent point.	You get disgusted.	You want to scream.	You decide to make it late if Dossible.
16.	Your friend fails to understand the solution to simple technical problem which you have explained many times over.	You tell your friend that he / she is stupid.	You continue totry.	You dismiss the subject.

Sr. No.	STATEMENT	a	b	c
17.	You are required to stay home to look after someone in your family and hence to cancel an outing.	You wouldn't doit.	You cancel your outing.	You look for an alternative solution.
18.	When you see a child being hit by its parent in public.	You sympathise with the child.	You get upset.	You look for an alternative solution.
19.	You are faced with a stiff problem.	'. can't solve it.	'm sure some thing will come up.	fhere can be no possible solution o this.
20.	Your friend arrives 45 minutes late for an appointment.	You are wild at him-/ her.	You refuse listen to excuses.	You ask for an explanation.
21.	You are asked to walk a long way to the market to get something for a party at home.	You refuse.	You agree to go.	You try, persuading other to go.
22.	If you see a blind man waiting try to cross a road and looking for help.	You want to see if someone else will help.	You immediately offer assistance.	You decide to ignore this situation.
23.	You have failed your examinations.	This is terrible.	I will always fail.	I'm sure I will do better next time.
24.	Caged birds are being sold all over the country.	You consider them decorative.	You appreciate their beauty.	You think that they ought to be freed.
25.	If you are asked to step down from some high post for a good cause.	You will resign.	You will fight and try to retain the post.	You will refuse it immediately.
26.	You are asked to baby sit a child for the evening.	You try to quickly put the child to sleep.	You try to forma rapport with the child.	You refuse to baby sit.
27.	You go for a movie with some family friends and find it very boring.	You wait till the end.	You walk out.	You tell your friend that they have bad taste.
28.	If you had to sacrifice a holiday for a friend's need.	You would go on your holiday.	You would help your friend out.	You tell your friends that they have bad taste.
29.	You see a man writing in pain on the roadside.	You help him.	You ignore him.	You can't help him but think about the incident for many days.
30.	You have been accused of a crime you never committed.	I will never be I will prove able to prove myself. My point.	I will prove my self.	There is no way I can get out of this.
31.	If you went home tired and found that you had to entertain some friends for the evening.	You display signs of reluctance.	You keep up a smile and ensure their comfort.	You will try your jest to give them a hint.

Sr. No.	STATEMENT	a	b	c
32.	Suppose you are a team captain and some discussion arose.	You would refuse to accept the views of other members.	You consider yourself supreme.	You believe in over all participation.
33.	If you finally find a dress you have been waiting for, for ages and discover that the size is not proper.	You wait for more places to arrive.	You buy it up any way and consider altering it.	You drop the idea completely.
34.	How would you react to the extreme poverty prevalent in slums?	Dirty slums sicken you.	You consider it their bad luck.	You feel responsible in some way.
35.	You are to play the lead role in play.	I can't act at all.	I am not presentable enough.	I will try and do my best.
36.	You are asked to attend a religious function at an old aunt's house.	You are unwelling because you dislike conventional people.	You accept just to please your aunt.	You can't hear to sit through long ceremonies.

PART - II

INSTRUCTIONS

From each of the following quotations, select the word that most accurately describes the mental state of the person making the statement. Cross out (X) the correct answer on the answer-sheet.

Sr. No.	STATEMENT	A	B	C
37.	The army will defend us. Will it?Won't it?	Despair	Indecision	Confidence
38.	And to think we had looked forward to this party for days.	Disappointment	Regret	Disgust
39.	We hate the way you admire her.What about us?	Despair	Jealousy	Possessiveness

PART-III

INSTRUCTIONS

In this part, *there are some statements regarding the way you behave and act. Each statement has a forced choice response of either 'yes' or 'No', try and decide whether 'Yes' or 'No' represents your usual way of behaving and acting. If yes, cross out (X) the cell below 'Yes' and if no, then cross out (X) the cell below 'No'.

40. If you were the host in a party and had to entertain a mixed crowd in which there were some people you disliked intensely would you gently avoid them and give the other more attention.
41. Your friend brings you a gift for some occasion and it so happens that you don't like it much, would you feelings obviously.
42. If you had to give someone a piece of bad news and after having searched for almost a day, you finally find him / her in a disturbed mood would you give the news?
43. On arriver for dinner at a friend's place you discover that none of the dishes prepared appeals to your appetite. Would you resist showing traces of disappointment.
44. In your various successful enterprises do you think that your opponents experiences strong sense of defeat.
45. Do you go through experiences where you find that in some controversial matter after a while your opponents willingly acknowledge your point of views.
46. If you are asked to intervene in an argument between two persons without supporting any of them, do you expect to be. successful.

PART IV

INSTRUCTIONS

Given below is a list of incomplete jokes. Against them, there are three choices with which to complete the joke. You are to select and cross out (X) the choice you consider to be the most humorous.

Sr. No.	STATEMENT	a	b	c
347.	Doctor to patients: 'Are you married by any chance?' Patients:	My wife chooses her own doctor.	No the reason I look this way is that I am sick.	That was ten years back.
48.	Two friends were discussing the reasons for their remaining single after all these years. 'Why only a few days', said the first, 'I met a girl and fell in love with her at first sight'. 'Well', then said the second, 'Why didn't you marry her'?	I took a second look.	She was my boss's wife.	Her boy-friends punched me.
49.	It was their first fight after marriage and the sordid subject was money. 'Before we were married', She cried, "You told me you were well off"	'So What' he yelled.	'I was', he snarled but I don't know it'.	How right I was he retorted.
50.	Why does he suffer from eyestrain?	Lack of spectacles	He lives opposite the YWCA	He sleeps very little
51	'You're a liar', challenged muscles, 'Really', grumbled the small man, 'Say that again and I'll burst your law' 'Consider it said', taunted muscles.	Forget it	Bye-bye, I have to hurry home	Consider it bursted.
52.	'Don't I look good tails?'	No.	We all do don't we.	Why not? Your ancestor did.
53.	Elderly passenger who objects to cigarette smoking. 'If you were my husband, I'd give you poison'. Replied the smoker:	Well if you were my wife I'd take it.	You'd still go to jail.	With or without desert.
54.	Patient to new doctor in the Mental Asylum, 'We all like your more than the old doctor';. 'Why?', queried the surprised doctor. The patient replied:	We feel you are more like one of us.	Well, the old doctor was longer. Slightly mad.	Your hair is was longer.

APPENDIX - II

Life Satisfaction Scale

Sr.No.	Statement	Always	Often	Sometime	Seldom	Never
1.	I set realistic goal for myself	☐	☐	☐	☐	☐
2.	I, on the whole, enjoy my life	☐	☐	☐	☐	☐
3.	I enjoy whatever I do.	☐	☐	☐	☐	☐
4.	I enjoy the way I five	☐	☐	☐	☐	☐
5.	I belief life is for living	☐	☐	☐	☐	☐
6.	I am satisfied with the subject I study	☐	☐	☐	☐	☐
7.	I feel that I am a successful person	☐	☐	☐	☐	☐
8.	I obtain pleasure from domestic affairs	☐	☐	☐	☐	☐
9.	I feel proud that I am successful in my Examination	☐	☐	☐	☐	☐
10.	I love to get myself involved in leisure activities	☐	☐	☐	☐	☐
11.	I feel happy when 1 achieve my goals	☐	☐	☐	☐	☐
12.	I am very much optimistic about my future	☐	☐	☐	☐	☐
13.	I feel my studies are less demanding	☐	☐	☐	☐	☐
14.	I think that I am self-made man	☐	☐	☐	☐	☐
15.	I set priorities by planning the day	☐	☐	☐	☐	☐
16.	I enjoy taking part in social activities	☐	☐	☐	☐	☐
17.	I devote some time to community activities	☐	☐	☐	☐	☐
18.	Money making is not the only motive of my life	☐	☐	☐	☐	☐
19.	want to make use of my skills to improve the quality of life	☐	☐	☐	☐	☐
20.	I want to raise my standard of living	☐	☐	☐	☐	☐
21.	I take life as it comes	☐	☐	☐	☐	☐
22.	I think I am capable of fulfilling demands of my life	☐	☐	☐	☐	☐
23.	I feel, I have a healthy sense of self	☐	☐	☐	☐	☐
24.	I hold optimistic attitude towards life	☐	☐	☐	☐	☐
25.	I maintain self-respect in different roles	☐	☐	☐	☐	☐
26.	I understand my strength and weaknesses	☐	☐	☐	☐	☐

27.	I believe in self-help and self-sufficiency	☐	☐	☐	☐	☐
28.	I have a lot of control over my life	☐	☐	☐	☐	☐
29.	I never leave a job unfinished	☐	☐	☐	☐	☐
30.	I am interested in sports activities	☐	☐	☐	☐	☐
31.	I can solve my problems effectively	☐	☐	☐	☐	☐
32.	I derive satisfaction from whatever I do	☐	☐	☐	☐	☐
33.	I believe I am a healthy person	☐	☐	☐	☐	☐
34.	I can face unanticipated hardships	☐	☐	☐	☐	☐
35.	I feel, I am a courageous person	☐	☐	☐	☐	☐

4. Creativity and Social Maturity of Teacher Trainees

1

The Problem and its Perspectives

INTRODUCTION

The importance of teaching thinking skills, including the ability to identify novel and effective solutions to unstructured problems, has long been considered an important goal for educators. It is particularly important for teacher educators who are seeking to prepare students. In the psychology literature a substantial body of research has been developed that specifically addresses the factors that can be managed to facilitate and motivate the creative process. The components, creativity relevant skills, domain relevant sills, and motivation, are identified as necessary and sufficient for creativity in any domain. The development of domain relevant skills, such as domain relevant knowledge and specific analytic tools, are identified as being important and with in the ambit of the teacher trainees.

THE CONCEPT OF CREATIVITY

The term creativity is widely used with reference to the creative people, the creative process, even a creative environment (Brown 1989). Our interest is in the process, culminating in a novel and effective solution to an open-ended problem. The importance of both novelty and effectiveness is reflected in the following definition. Creativity is the ability to produce work that is both novel and appropriate (Sternberg 1988). This definition is widely accepted in the creativity literature (Amabile 1966; Sternberg 1999). However, environmental factors will interact with individual differences and influence the creative process (Amabile 1996). Focusing on the process, and the facts that will influence that process, highlighting the implications for addressing heuristic (open-ended) problems within a teaching course in ways that support the creative process. Guilford (1950) made an important contribution to our understanding of creativity when he distinguished between convergent and divergent thinking processes. Convergent thinking is similar to conventional notions of intelligence in which existing knowledge / information is synthesized to arrive at the single most appropriate answer. Guilford argued that creativity is expressed in terms of divergent thinking, however this led to measuring creativity in terms of the number of fundamentally different solutions that were generated (e.g., Torrance 1974). This emphasis on divergent thinking and novelty is consistent with the typical layperson's conception of creativity.

Many of the theorists who have modeled the creative process incorporate both divergent and convergent thinking processes. There is a role for divergent thinking in order to recognize previously unnoticed problems and in exploring possible responses. However, convergent thinking is also important as relevant information is identified and brought to bear on the problem. The recognition that both divergent and convergent thinking is important in the creative process is important for educators because the way in which problems are presented and evaluated will have an impact on a student's thinking process. The following sections describe the creative process and consider the implications for facilitating and motivating Guilford (1950) made an important contribution to our understanding of creativity when he distinguished between convergent and divergent thinking processes. Convergent thinking is similar to conventional notions of intelligence in which existing knowledge / information is synthesized to arrive at the single most appropriate answer. Guilford argued that creativity is expressed in terms of divergent thinking, however this led to measuring creativity in terms of the number of fundamentally different solutions that were generated that process in the classroom.

THE CREATIVE PROCESS

Creativity was initially studied as an intellectual or personality trait. The emphasis was on the creative individual and the nature of creativity was considered to be a black box' (Barron and Harrington 1981). More recently, however, there have been various attempts to describe and model the creative process so that it can then be effectively managed.

Amabile (1996) describes four phases in the creative process, namely: 1. Problem identification, 2. Preparation, 3. Response generation, and 4.Validation and communication. Other theorists describe similar phases, for example, preparation, incubation, illumination, and verification (Wallas 1926) on preparation, Production, evaluation, and implementation (Hogarth 1980). In this section Amabil's model of the creative process is presented to provide a context for the subsequent discussion of motivating and facilitating creativity in the classroom. Amabil's model was chosen because she has devoted particular attention to the positive effect that expected evaluation and rewards can have when applied appropriately to the various phases of the creative process. The first step in the creative process is to identify that a problem exists (Runco and Chand 1994). The problem may be presented to the individual, or recognition that a problem exists may be generated internally. Getzels and Csikszentmihallyi (1976) suggest that 'discovered problems' are more likely to be solved creatively than 'presented problems'. Furthermore, always presenting the student with a predetermined problem ignores the importance of problem identification skills.

Problem based learning emphasizes the importance of student's identifying the problem for themselves whereas case studies tend to be more focused and direct the student to address specific issues / problems. The importance of identifying and responding to the root cause of a problem rather than symptoms may be the most important determinant of successful innovation in schools.

As noted by Thomas (1999) problem symptoms are often mistakenly identified as problems, resulting in waste efforts at solving something that was not a problem. Through appropriate instruction students can develop the skills necessary to think beyond sterepriate instruction students can develop the skills necessary to think beyond stereotypical conceptions of the problem. When a problem has been identified, preparation includes building up or reactivating relevant information. The way in which an individual combines and reorganizes information in the preparation phase plays a crucial role in the generation of responses. Finke, Ward and Smith (1992) note that the combination and reorganization efforts can bring new features to the forefront that may lead to a reconceptualisation of the initial problem. Therefore, the problem may be redefined, leading to a very different solution, depending on the way in which the information is analyzed.

Amabile (1996) notes that this is one of the 'perspiration' phases of the creative process that individuals may seek to bypass, moving too quickly to the more intrinsically motivating idea generation phase. The response generation phase determines the extent to which the solution will be novel. Moving too quickly through this phase may limit the number of possible responses since obvious ideas is usually generated first, and, only when these are exhausted, more remote association are found (Runco and Sakamoto 1999). Here the ability to suspend critical judgment is important. Brainstorming (Osborn 1953) is one technique that has been proposed to increase the number of responses. It involves creating a non-threatening atmosphere to avoid inhibitions. The final solution will be chosen from the ideas that have been generated. While there is some support (Milgram and Rabkin 1978) for a positive relationship between the quantity and quality of responses, the quality of responses generated will also be determined by the level of understanding of the problem space.

FACTORS INFLUENCING THE CRATIVE PROCESS

Amabile (1983) argues that creativity is best conceptualized not as a personality Trait or as a general ability, but as a behavior resulting from particular constellations of personal characteristics, cognitive abilities, and social environments. This view was shared by most contemporary theorists (Mumford et.al 1993) who emphasize changing the environment in order to promote and facilitate creativity. It is particularly relevant for educators wishing to establish an environment that supports creativity by managing the factors that promote or inhibit it. Amabil's componential model of creativity specifically recognizes the importance of domain-relevant skills, motivation and creativity relevant skills.

EDUCATION AND SOCIETY

Education is the fulcrum upon which hangs the peaceful evolutionary transition of Society. It plays a vital role in building a society. A modern society cannot achieve its aim of economic growth, technical development and cultural advancement without fully harnessing the talents of its citizens. For the advancement in education proper social maturity, values and adjustment pattern should be there. Social maturity, values and adjustment pattern should be there. Social maturity is related to values that are found in the society. Teacher educators are very well associated with the cultivation of social maturity among the student teachers. Then only they will develop an integrated personality, proper cultivation of values to cope with the environment amicably.

Man doesn't stand-alone; he is only and essentially a social animal, otherwise he may describe as a "beast" or a "god" but not as a "man". Similarly society is just an abstraction unless it mirrors the human values, norms, ambitions and goals society is never an aggregate of individuals. It's, in the sense, no predictable string of unity. Tandra Patanic (1986) states, "The society is rather a peculiar amalgamation of unity and diversity, which characterizes the society that again reflects the nature of human mind" (p.40). Mind can be judged from various sensitivity and emotionality. Separately none of these qualities of the mind can be called to constitute the proper essence of the mind. So man and the society and their relation have been viewed here as a prism throwing multi-colored spectrum of light. Yet the arrangement of colour may change in the direction of the light. Society is a prism; it has multiple facets along with its unique ability of adapting to the changes of circumstances.

EDUCATION AS AN AGENCY OF SOCIETY

The process of education is of deep significance to the growth and welfare of society. If the people are to keep pace with the fast changing social order, with scientific discoveries and with the explosion of knowledge in all parts of the world, the hidden talents of youth must be brought to the surface and be exploited for the good of the society. There is a great demand for creative ideas and creative talents, and education is the best means for the developments of such talents. The events of our time are moving continually, accelerating the rate and if the people are to keep pace with them, the people must make sure that the talents of the youth are thoroughly developed.

Alexander. A. Schaeiders (1965) defines "Education is the total experiences that can transform the life of the individual person". Education can contribute much and in many different ways to the social, moral and religious growth of the adolescent to healthy social perspectives to adequate vocational attitudes and goals, and to the future roles that the adolescent will expect to play. By means of active participation on the playing field and through extracurricular activities such as oratory, debating, newspaper reporting or yearbook editing the adolescent can pick up many ideas, skills and general know-how that may be of great help to him later in his social relations and vocational aspirations.

MATURITY AS A DETERMINANT OF PERSONALITY

Henery. E. Garett (2968) says, "Social maturity is the degree of social participation as Measured by child's activities, attitudes and play interests. It is related to physical growth and maturity and to mental ability". One of the components of social maturity is adjustment. Maturity is the determinant of personality. A man's personality is the total picture of his organized behavior, especially as it can be characterized by his fellow men in a consistent way.

An individual, since his birth attempts to interest with his environment. Behavior of an individual can be defined as an adjustment to his environment. Every individual develops his own unique way of adjustment in the society. Socially matured individuals are better able to adjust to the various changes in the environment and react appropriately, thus making the right type of adjustment.

MPORTANCE OF MATURITY

Nazarth Maria E. Waples (1978) defines, "Maturity is the blossoming of man's Character into a unified totality. It discerns the processes that contribute to the psychological and physical growth and well-being of man".

Maturity assumes accountability, constantly assesses, judges and taken appropriate decisions. Maturity develops a balanced emotional outlook, helping the individual to accept himself, his talents and limitation and to accept others as they are. It analyses values and internalized them consistently. It helps towards progressive advancement in spiritual growth, impelling the individual to adapt himself to change and to life without emotional crises. Abraham Sperling (1967) states social maturity in the following words "An adolescent should get along with and well with others. He ought to develop self-reliance in matters of taste and ought to develop tolerance of human differences." Maturity is gradual process that comes with self-knowledge and with self-realization shaping man into a responsible adult.

CHARACTERISTICS OF SOCIALLY MATURED INDIVIDUAL

Social maturity is evidenced in the capacity of the individual to maintain Friendships that meet the needs of others as well as his own. Vatsysyan (1990) states "A mature individual from the social stand point is one who co-operates with all those with whom be comes into contact and contradicts them only when such a course of actions becomes inevitable. He is never ill-mannered choosing instead to appear very well mannered, considerate and friendly to all and sundry" (P.119), consequently has a large circle of friends. An adult, who has attended that stage as required by the standpoint, evinces great interest in art, study, games etc.

He studies the works of greatest authors and taken interest in games and forms of recreation suitable to his station in life. His activities and conduct are scrupulously in conformity with his age and sex. He has the power of independent decision and judgment. He gives every evidence of being well balanced and adjusted with himself and his behavior towards other individuals.

Elizabeth B.Hurlock (1959) says, "The socially mature individual has a sense of his proper place and role as a member of a group. He is willing and able to orient himself in the various activities with others and customs of the group, to make the proportionate contribution to the work to be done, to take a suitable part in the social exchange to assume a reasonable amount of responsibility and to adjust himself to the inevitable limitations and restrictions of community life without waste of energy or loss of satisfaction." He can be original and yet conform to the broad pattern of the cultural environment.

Taneja R.P. (1989) says, "Social maturity refers to degree of growth in social and vocational abilities." The Socially mature individual treats the members of his family as friends. In this role he shows the affection, loyalty, consideration and respect for all family members. As a citizen the socially mature person accepts his obligations and performs them faithfully. He makes good adjustments to all types of people without prejudice based on their religion, race or skin colour.

The matured accepts his friends as they are and does not criticize or try to change them as a socially immature person does. He is loyal to them and feels a sense of responsibility towards them when they need his help. Although social life may add greatly to his happiness, the mature person is self-sufficient enough that he can be happy when circumstances make it possible for him to be with his family, friends or acquaintances.

The mature individual can be found to possess the trait of good humour and pleasantness. The important point is that he keeps himself alive, with vigorous interests that make him interesting to be with. The mature individual possess a feeling of social concern and gets very involved in situations that call for obedience to social norms too. The person equipped with the human sensitivities that make for maturity will usually have powerful concern with social problems and ways of alleviating them. For all his savoring of human relationships, the maturing individual is not dependent on always having company.

The mature person knows that he has to go on choosing alternatives, that each alternative costs him something, and there are things he will never be able to do and experience. He also knows that there are things he will never be able to do again, that he can never recapture his youth or relive his first encounters with certain experiences. He knows that his integrity is continually threatened by practical demands, by seductive temptations, by concessions and compromises, by conflicting values, and can only real rewards in life come with continued growth, and that there is no room in the one material life he has for major regrets. This individual who has approached maturity can know that he has loved, had loved, had done his work, and has made his mark on people.

STATEMENT OF THE PROBLEM

The Problem is titled *"CREATIVITY AND SOCIAL MATURITY OF TEACHER TRAINEES."*

SIGNIFICANCE OF THE STUDY

Social maturity can only be found through self-knowledge and self - control, based on the objective existence of a science of human nature. In order to protect socially supported beliefs and conventions, society employs a complex system of prohibitions, backed up by ostracism and punishment.

Society sets up a system of socially convenient belief for truth, and conventional patterns of behavior for what are right. The individual who chooses to live outside this system has two fold tasks, to make his peace with society at adaptive level, and to maintain always his own independent standards of what a high quality life is all about. To accomplish this end he must be able to see what is compulsive or obsessive in himself, working to reduce or eliminate these influences in his life without losing track of the wisdom and strength he already has. His motivation for doing this is the promotion of his own mental health there is no ostracism, only selective withdrawal, and no punishment, only selective indifference. Identity is carried by their devotion to the quality of living for themselves and others, and is not invested in career success, ethnic identity, or in their ability to survive through coping with recurrent psychological crises.

Social maturity is the final expected outcome of social development. The socially matured person knows his role as a member of the social group. The person will organize himself socially and will take part in various activities and customs of the group. A person with high social maturity will know the responsibilities and will be able to adjust himself in the society as he would have good creativity so as to solve the problems of the students. So it is significant to study the social maturity and creativity of the secondary grade teacher trainees, as it is essential for the classroom teaching and effective interaction.

OBJECTIVES OF THE STUDY

1. To find out the significance of difference in the fluency level of men and women teacher trainees.
2. To find out the significance of difference in the flexibility level of men and women teacher trainees.
3. To find out the significance of difference in the originality level of men of women teacher trainees.
4. To find out the significance of difference in the personal adequacy of men and women teacher trainees.
5. To fine out the significance of difference in the interpersonal adequacy of men and women teacher trainees.

6. To find out the significance of difference in the social adequacy of men and women teacher trainees.
7. To find out of the significance of difference in the social maturity of men and women teacher trainees.
8. To find out the significance of difference between teacher trainees studying in Government and Government Aided institutions with respect to fluency level.
9. To find out the significance of difference between teacher trainees studying in Government and Government Aided institutions with respect to flexibility level.
10. To find out the significance of difference between teacher trainees studying in Government and Government Aided institutions with respect to originality level.
11. To find out the significance to difference between teacher trainees studying in Government and Government Aided institutions with respect to personal adequacy in social maturity.
12. To find out the significance of difference between teacher trainees studying in Government and Government Aided institutions with respect to Interpersonal adequacy in social maturity.
13. To find out the significance of difference between teacher trainees studying in Government and Government Aided institutions with respect to social adequacy in social maturity.
14. To find out the significance of difference between teacher trainees studying in Government and Government Aided institutions with respect to overall social maturity.
15. To find out the significance of difference between teacher trainees studying in first year and second year with respect to fluency level in creativity.
16. To find out the significance of difference between teacher trainees studying in first year and second year with respect to flexibility level in creativity.

17. To find out the significance of difference between teacher trainees studying in first year and second year with respect to originality level in creativity.
18. To find out the significance of difference between teacher trainees studying in first year and second year with respect to personal adequacy in the social maturity scale.
19. To find out the significance of difference between teacher trainees studying in first year and second year with respect to interpersonal adequacy in the social maturity scale.
20. To find out the significance of difference between teacher trainees studying in first year and second year with respect to social adequacy in the social maturity scale.
21. To find out the significance of difference between teacher trainees studying in first year and second year with respect to overall social maturity.
22. To find out the significance of difference between the teacher trainees in the creativity factors based on their father's qualifications.
23. To find out the significance of difference between the teacher trainees in the social maturity based on their father's qualifications.
24. To find out the significance of difference between the teacher trainees in the creativity factors based on their mother's qualifications.
25. To find out the significance of difference between the teacher trainees in the social maturity based on their mother's qualifications.
26. To find out the significance of difference between the teacher trainees in the creativity factors based on their parental income.
27. There is significant relationship between creativity dimensions and personal adequacy of teacher trainees.
28. There is significant relationship between creativity dimensions and interpersonal adequacy of teacher trainees.
29. There is significant relationship between creativity dimensions and social adequacy of teacher trainees.

30. There is significant relationship between creativity dimensions and social maturity of teacher trainees.
31. There is significant relationship between creativity dimensions and social maturity of teacher trainees.

CONCLUSION

The first chapter is chiefly concerned with the conceptual frame work of the problem. The discussion on creativity and has been presented to highlight the conceptual position with which this study has been placed and conducted. Having acquainted with the necessary theoretical aspects of social maturity and creativity the investigator has reviewed the related research conducted by the educational experts in India and abroad. The summary of related literature is presented in the next chapter.

2

Review of Related Literature

INTRODUCTION

An essential part of research project is the review of studies related to the present investigation. The terms 'Review' means revision or glance over, or refer back on. Review of research studies pertaining to the problem under investigation is of fundamental importance. The present chapter summarizes research studies related to the problem "CREATIVITY AND SOCIAL MATURITY OF TEACHER TRAINEES."

STUDIES ON CREATIVITY

INDIAN STUDIES

Dubey Sushma (1986) investigated into the Educational influences on development of Creative thinking in children. It was assumed that there is a symbolize relationship between natural / social environment and creative thinking. The hypotheses of the study were; there will be positive association between age and creative thinking there will be positive association between enriched school education environment and creative thinking and there will be positive association between enriched family environment and creative thinking.

The sample consisted of 255 male students (130 from an enriched school education environment and 125 from an impoverished school education environment) The tools administered were kuppuswamy's Scocio Economic status scale, Baquer Mehdi's Non verbal Test of Creative Thinking and Passi's Puzzle test. The data obtained were subjected to multifactor analysis of variance, correlation analysis and factor analysis. The major findings were Age, School, Education environment; family education environment and socio class were found to have significant positive main effects on creative thinking in children. The interaction between age and space, space and school education environment, and school education environment and family education environment had significant effect on creative thinking.

Golwalkar (1986) in his study on the scientific attitude, creativity and achievement used a sample of 270 tribal non-tribal students of Rajestan studying in classes IX and X offering science as an optional subject.

The main objectives of the research were to study the scientific attitude of tribal and non-tribal students, to compare the creativity of tribal and non-tribal students and to compare the achievement of tribal and non-tribal students in science subjects.

The tools were Scientific Attitude Scale, Thinking Creativity with words and Thinking Creativity with figures. Analysis of data revealed that: non-tribals were found to be superior to tribals on three components of scientific attitude, the non-tribals had a higher level of creativity than the tribals and the non-tribal students had a higher level of scholarly achievement in science subjects than the tribal students.

Desai (1987) investigated into the creative thinking ability of students of higher secondary of Gujarat state in the context of some psycho-socio factors. The objective was to study the creative thinking ability in relation to scholastic achievement, anxiety and reasoning ability. The sample consisted of 608 students. Analysis of data revealed that: there was no difference in creative thinking ability of urban and rural higher secondary students, the students with higher scholastic achievement were found better in creative thinking than students with scholastic achievement and the students with good reasoning ability were better in creative thinking than students with poor reasoning ability.

Raina (1986) investigated into psychosocial correlates of scientific creativity among high school students. The aims of the study were to find out the relationship between scientific creativity and achievement in science for boys and girls, to study the effect of sex and type of school on scientific creativity among high school students, to study the effect of socio economic status, sex problem solving ability and achievement in science on scientific creativity and to study the effect of sex, birth order and type of family on scientific creativity.

The tools administered on a sample of 1000 students (459 boys and 541 girls) were the Gupta Scientific Creativity Test, Achievement Test in Science and the Socio Economic Status scale.

The noted findings were Achievement in science was significantly related with scientific creativity, the mean scientific creativity score of high achievers in science was more than that of middle and low achievers. Middle achievers were more creative than low achievers in science, first - born students were more creative in science than second and third borne and students belonging to middle socio economic status and having high achievement scores were highest in scientific creativity.

Trimurthy (1987) investigated into the Creative Thinking Ability of Secondary school students in the context of some Psych-socio Factors. The objectives of the study were to study the trends of creative thinking ability in relation to age and to study the relationship of socio economic status with creative thinking ability.

The sample consisted of 603 secondary school students. Results indicated that: boys were better than the girls in both verbal and non-verbal creative thinking ability and urban students were better than the rural students in both verbal and non-verbal creative thinking ability students with high IQ were found to be more creative than students with low IQ in verbal creative thinking ability.

FOREIGN STUDIES

The effect of intelligence, creativity, and cognitive style on success in composition was studied by Meduffie, Harriet E. (1988). This is a descriptive study of 109 college freshmen at a small southern public university which used the Torrance Tests of Creative Thinking Verbal (TTCT), the Otis-Lennon School Abilities Test (OLSAT), and the Cognitive Style Map (CSM), and an average score of two Writing Samples to obtain a composite portrait of a successful academic writer. The findings of the study demonstrate that students with high performance scores in writing are more affected by intelligence and cognitive style than by creativity. In fact, creativity scores on originality had no co relational significance with success in academic writing performance.

Keith James (1991) investigated Personality, Cognitive Skills, and Creativity in Different Life Domains. A preliminary effort was made to integrate personality and cognitive-skill approaches to understanding the sources of creativity. It was proposed that personality and cognitive skill each have differential predicative power for different types (i.e., domains) of creativity. Further, it was proposed that cognitive skills at least partially mediate personality effects on creativity and that personality and cognitive skills may interact to shape creativity. Both personality and divergent thinking measures were used to predict 3 types of creativity-problem solving, artistic, and social-among 41 students in a creativity course. Results of bivariate correlation, analysis of variance, and regression analyses provided some support for the ideas that (a) different types of creativity are somewhat independent of each other, (b) personality and divergent thinking have somewhat different relations to creativity of different types, (c)originality of thinking partially medicates the relations of personality to creativity in different domains, and (d) personality and divergent thinking have some interactive, as well as some main effect, impacts on creativity.

Weinerman, Ilene (1997) conducted a study on creativity in the classroom; an examination of student teacher personality and perceptions of the classroom setting (preservice). The Purpose of this study was to identify the positive and negative relationship between creativity and personality, as well as the direction and degree of association among creativity, personality, and the student teacher's classroom emphasis and orientation. An additional purpose was the development and testing of a path model to determine whether causal linkages can be established among these same sets of variables. Specifically examined were the direct effects of personality and creativity, as well as the significance of creativity as an intervening variable with indirect effect on perceptions of the classroom setting.

Singh (1986) assessed achievement motivation, level of aspiration, and anxiety as correlates of creativity among denitrified tribal (DT) children. The author compared 450 denitrified tribe children and 450 students from ashram-type and general schools. In view of the lower level of functioning of DT children the author suggested formal education from the nursery stage for them; more of vocational and physical facilities, scope for inter-personal relationships, and psycho-educational guidance programmes. Admission of normal children to ashram schools would provide a cultural mix.

Seventy-eight student teachers enrolled in the teacher certification program at Fordham University completed three measures of personality, creativity, and classroom perceptions. Person correlations and path analyses were used to analyze the data.

Results indicated that student teachers who maintained a student-centered classroom focus tended to have high needs for affiliation and endurance, with low needs for cognitive structure, aggression, and harm avoidance. These same individuals also evidenced high scores on measures of creativity. More creative student teachers tended to have low needs for social recognition and structure. Five path models were generated based upon the pattern of intercorrelations obtained.

Although personality and creativity were found to have some significant direct effects on classroom focus, personality was not found to have an indirect effect mediated by any of the creativity variables. The independent variables accounted for between 10% and 22% of the variance in classroom focus, indicating the need to consider additional variables for inclusion in future studies in order to improve the predictive power of the model.

Hieberger (1983), on a sample of elementary school students studied about the effects of two Creativity Training Programmes upon the Creativity and Achievement of Young, Intellectually gifted student. Guilford's structure of Intellect (SI) model which was designed in 1959 has been utilized in the study of creativity. Analysis of data using tests and Analysis of covariance revealed that students in Creativity Programme A experienced greater gain than did-students in Creativity Programme B. The achievement level decreased on both sub tests.

Scott (1984) investigated into the influence of Home environment on the development of Creativity in third through fifth grade children. The Problem under investigation was to determine how the home environments of the more creative and less creative child differ. To identify the elements in the home environment that may relate to the child's creativity. To determine the correlation between the home environment and Creativity, mothers of the children tested were administered a 150 questions interview schedule. The results showed that creative children were found differ from non-creative children at a statistically significant level in three areas, variety of intellectual / cultural activities in the home extent of the child's creative activities and flexibility in the household.

Orieux (1989) on a sample 157 grade eleven students (81 males and 76 females) studies about correlated of Creative Ability and Performance. Creative Ability was assessed with the Wallach kongan divergent thinking tests and Creative performance was assessed from three sources: the creative Activities Checklist

(Runeo and Albeert 1985), completed by students. The teacher's Evaluation of students' Creativity and the Parent's Evaluation of Student's Creativity. Correctional analysis were conducted to determine the relationship of the creativity measures with intellectual ability, assessed with a group intelligence test and academic achievement obtained from school records data. The major findings were performances were significantly related to intellectual ability and academic achievement at moderate to low levels. Multivariate analyses of variance conducted to evaluate gender effect for all measures reveled that females significantly differ from males.

Females obtaining higher mean scores on two achievement measures.

Howell (1990) studied the relationship between Arts education and Creativity among High School Students. The purpose of the study was to examine possible difference between mean creativity scores of subjects, from High Schools with varying arts education experience, Arts disciplines and degree of Academic Achievement. The tool employed for data collection was Torrance Test of Creative Thinking (TTCT). Analysis of data using one way and two-way ANOVAs revealed that three were tendencies for subjects with the highest TTCT scores to have the highest academic achievement scores. A female in all arts disciplines to score higher than males on TTCT.

Onenye, (1991) investigated into the relationship between the cognitive dimensions of Creativity and Future Time Perspective (FTP). The purpose of the study was to investigate the relationship between the cognitive dimensions of creativity and Future Time Perspective. An attempt was made to investigate Guilford's cognitive model of Creativity with Nurmi's problem solving model of Future Time Perspective. The sample consisted of 135 female Under Graduate Students between the ages 18024. Tools administrated were Guildford's Consequences for measuring Creativity and Future Problem Solving Tasks instrument. The findings were consequences and Future Problem Solving Tasks were significantly correlated on all the creativity variables considered. Creativity was found to be stronger predictor of future time Perspective than academic achievement.

Kin (1993) studied the relationship of creativity measures to School Achievement and Preferred Learning and Thinking Style in a sample of 193 Korean High School Students. The Creativity constructs were operationalized in terms of scores on selected measures taken from the Torrance Test of Creative Thinking (TTCT). The statistical techniques used Person's Product moment Correlation Coefficients, t-tests and Analysis of Variance. The major findings were measures of Creativity translated from the Torrance Test of Creative Thinking (TTCT) show little, in any, relationship to School achievement. Korean High School females may be expected to exhibit higher average levels of performance on creativity tests than their male counter parts.

Bisset (1996) investigated into the relationship of Creativity and Achievement to performance of middle School students in solving real world science problems. Tools administered on a sample of fourteen groups of seventh-grade students were the Torrance Creative Problem Solving Figural Test and California Achievement Test. Analysis of data revealed that both creativity and achievement and indicators of success in-group problem solving of ill-structured problems. Creativity reflected greater significance than group achievement on the California Achievement test, as an indicator of success in problem solving on the undersea city Design problem.

Baues Ann Leslie (1995) investigated "Helping children to Maturity Measuring the effect of participation in a pear facilitation project on sixth graders self-esteem, social maturity and patterns of social choice." This research explored the question whether the affective benefits associates with participating in peer facilitation can be empirically measured. Much of the literature concerning peer facilitation can be empirically measured. Much of the literature concerning peer facilitation has discussed the affective benefits of participation and proposed theoretical explanations for those benefits. The most common kind of support for those claims has been anecdotal in nature.

The population chosen for the study was rural mainstream sixth grade students. They were divided into a control group (N=9) and treatment groups. Treatment group 1 (N=30) had high school student group leaders and Treatment group 2 (N=25) had adult group leaders. The sixth grades were trained for 10 weeks in active listening skills and then matched with kindergarten students completed 15 development pay lessons.

Pre and post measurements were collected concerning self-esteem Rosonberg self Esteem Scale, (1965). Interpersonal development skills - Beset and Palomares, (1970). Socimetric patterns of choice - COMPSOC Tread well and Saxton, (1993). "T" tests were calculated to determine changes by group and by gender. Significant results were found for self-esteem and for some choice patterns.

Results for interpersonal skills were unclear and some choice patterns were not affected. In addition adult professional group leadership was found to be more beneficial than group leadership. Some significant differences were found for gender. Several sub-hypothesis were tested involving the relationship between self-esteem popularity and empathy and some significant results were found. Sociograms were drawn pre and post for each group and the implications of the patterns that emerged were discussed at the Marco and Micro level.

STUDIES ON SOCIAL MATURITY

INDIAN STUDIES

GHOSH. S (1975) studied the social maturity of per school age Bengali children of Calcutta city belonging to different socio-economic groups. The major objectives where to construct a scale for the appraisal of social maturity. To determine social maturity on the basis of the social quotient distribution of the sample concerned. To certify the value of social quotient in predicting the intelligence quotient. To apply the scale for appraisal of social maturity of normal (longitudinal study) and different clinical groups.

Sings of age wise social growth and the characteristic pattern of behaviour expressing age wise social maturity were studied and on the basis of the findings, a scale for the appraisal of Social maturity, viz., a Social Maturity Inventory was constructed.

Thirty-six, nursery and kindergarten schools were randomly selected from the different regions of Calcutta and 40 pre-school children (20 boys and 20 Girls) were selected ROM each school at random equally distributed in each age group. Data were also collected by using a standardized interview schedule on the mother of these selected children. The final sample included 1410 cases.

Social age scores and social quotients (SQ) were found out for all the children. The reliability, predictability validity and norms for the inventory were established. The capacity of the scale for the clientele was testified. Possible deviations were determined. Influential modes that might affect the growth sign of social behavior and there by the social quotient of a child were looked for. The study revealed that sex had very insignificant as testimony of ability to enrich the social maturity level. Social competency was the consequence of acculturation feedback, irrespective of any training or controlled environment. The instrument was highly reliable and valid. The derived equation for determining social maturity was found.

Agnihotri, C.S. (1991) has conducted a cross cultural comparative study between tribal and non tribal first generation and traditional learners in relation to their social maturity and educational adjustment. The sample consisted of 113 first generation tribal learners and 108 traditional tribal learners. Social maturity was independent of traditions of learning. The tribal and non-tribal differed in terms of their placements on attribute of social maturity. The traditions of learning were found to be contributing to social maturity. It was found that, the social maturity and educational adjustment were only social ingredients. Psychological characteristics also influenced the social ingredients. Psychological characteristics also influenced the social maturity and educational adjustment of children and social maturity was independent of traditions of learning.

Bhushan, A. (1994) conducted a study on social maturity across sex and family vocations. The sample comprised of 200 student teachers from two colleges, equally divided between two sexes. Major variable used were sex values, and family vocations. The tools used for data collections were the form D of value survey. The study highlights, male and female uniformly assigned highest importance to social maturity. Both male and female from service and non-service class had politeness as a subdivision on their maturity.

Puranki, S.D (1985) investigated the relationship of social maturity of pupils with organizational climate and Teacher's morale in the primary schools of Bangalore city. The study was conducted to find out the levels of social maturity of male and female students separately. The levels of social maturity of male and female students separately. The levels of social maturity of students under the influence of selected independent variables. The relationship between social maturity of students on the one hand and organizational climate and morale of teachers on the other. Morale of male and female teachers separately. Morale of teachers under different variables. The sample of the study included 70 schools 2634 students and 712 teachers.

The tools used for the study were Thirtha's social maturity scale, Sharma's organizational climate Descriptive Questionnaire and the Teacher's Morale scale designed by the investigator. The statistical techniques used were one-way ANOVA, co-efficient of correlation and 't' test.

The major findings were that the social maturity level of female students was higher than that of male students. In the development of social maturity, autonomous climate, private management and unaided schools and urban location of schools were found to be most conductive factors. The morale of female teachers was higher than that of male teachers. The controlled organizational climate, government, management and urban locality were conductive to development of morale of teachers. No single dimension of organizational climate was effective for the development of social maturity of students. Morale of all teachers who formed the subjects of study was found to be non-effective in contributing to the development of social maturity of their students. No effect of morale of teachers of both sexes was noticed on the development of social maturity of male of female students or on the students of both sexes even under the influence of organizational climates, school organizations and localities.

FOREIGN STUDIES

Pattramon Jumpangern (1986) studied the Social Maturity of Teachers-college students of western region of Thailand, in the context of some psycho-socio factors.

The major objectives were to prepare a reliable and valid tool to measure social maturity. To study the social maturity of teacher-college students of the western region of Thailand coming from urban and rural areas. To study the social maturity of teacher-college students of different sex. To study the social maturity of the teachers-college students of different age groups. To study the social maturity of the teachers-college students in the context of their SES. To study the social maturity of the teachers-college students in the context of certain personality trains namely, Dominance Vs Submission, Leadership, Radicalism Vs Conventionalism, Neuroticism, Emotional Stability and Suggestibility. To study the social maturity of student teachers in relation to their personal, social and family adjustment.

For collecting the data for maturity the researcher constructed a social maturity scale by following the mixed model technique. Initially 95 statements were constructed keeping in view the behavior of socially matured individuals. Our of these statements, by applying various techniques of item discrimination. 60 statements were selected for final from. The age norms were established over a sample 669. The reliability of the scale established by various methods ranged between 0.78 and 0.92. The concept and concurrent validity were established. The other tools used for collecting data were SES by A.A. Patel and Personality Inventory by A.S. Patel.

For studying social in relation to certain personality traits, a 2*2*3 factorial design was used. Analysis of variance was used for verifying the hypotheses.

The teachers - college students coming from urban areas were found to be more matured than those coming from rural areas. The male student teachers were found superior to the female student teachers. The student teachers of age group 25-29 were more matured than student teacher of age group 17-20 and 21-24. The student teachers with high SES were more socially matured than those low SES. Students with dominance personality traits were more socially matured than those having submissive personality traits. Students have high leaderships traits were more socially matured than those having low leadership traits. "Students having radicalism personality traits were more socially matured than those having conventionalist traits. Students having low neuroticism were socially matured than those having high neuroticism.

Students having emotional stability were more matured than those having low emotional stability. Students having good family adjustment were more socially matured than those having poor family adjustment. Students having good personal adjustment were more socially matured than those having poor personnel social adjustment.

Banes Ann Leslie (1995) conducted a study on measuring of effect of participation in a peer facilitation project on sixth graders self esteem, social maturity and patterns of social choice. The population chosen for the study was rural mainstream sixth grade students. The sample was tested by Socimetric pattern of choice. It was found that some significant difference in social maturity for gender and there was significant relationship between self-esteem and social maturity.

Savluk Thongngamkahom., (1983) studied the social maturity as a function of some psycho-socio adjustments factors of B.Ed., college students of North-central region f Thailand. The major objectives were to prepare a reliable and valid to measure social maturity. To study the social maturity of B.Ed., college students in the North-Central region of Thailand. To study the Social Maturity of B.Ed., college students coming from single sex schools and mixed schools. To compare Social Maturity of B.Ed., college students of different sexes. To study the Social Maturity of B.Ed., college students with regard to their socio-economic status. To study the social Maturity of B.Ed., college students with regard to their socio-economic status. To study the Social Maturity in relation to personal social adjustment. To study the Social Maturity in relation to family adjustment.

The sample of the study included 922 students, including boys and girls from the North-Central region. The social maturity scale was prepared by following the Likert method. The scale was standardized on a sample of 922 students, including boys and girls from the North-Central region. The reliability, validity and norms of the scale were established. For measuring SES and personality traits. A.S/Patel's SES scale and personality inventory were translated into English and that were used for collecting the data. The reliability of the scale, as established by different method ranged between 0.84 and 0.92. The concurrent validity established by correlating the scores on the scale with teacher's opinion about maturity was found to be 0.73. The 2x2x2 factorial design and analysis of variance technique was used for arriving at conclusion.

The major findings were that the B.Ed., college students with high SES background were found more socially matured that those of coming from low SES strata. The students having dominant personality trait were more socially matured than those of having submissive personality trait. The students having high leadership personality trait were more socially matured than those of having low leadership personality trait. The students having radicalism personality trait were more socially matured than those having conventionalist personality trait. The students having low neuroticism were more socially matured than those having high neuroticism. The students having high emotional maturity were more socially matured than those having suggestibility and low suggestibility traits neither did not differ on social maturity. The students having good social adjustment were more socially matured than those having poor personal social adjustment. The students having good family adjustment were found to be more socially matured than those with poor family adjustment.

CONCLUSION

From the above description of the creativity and social maturity, the investigator has understood the need for the full-fledged studies on creativity and social maturity. In most of the studies the researchers used the standardized tools only. From the analysis it has been found that there is no study related to creativity and social maturity was conducted. Social maturity and creativity are very much needed for the teacher trainees. So the investigator has selected this topic for his research work.

3

Methodology

INTRODUCTION

Research is always directed towards solution to some problems. It develops the curiosity about the unknown and it is a procedure from known to unknown. The ultimate goal of any research work is to find out the cause and effect relationship between the variables. Educational research is concerned with the development and testing theories of how students behave in the educational setting. The success of an educational research depends on the systematic adoption of the scientific method. A research process so implemented would enhance the validity and reliability of the research.

RESEARCH METHODS

A research method is a systematic process of collecting and analyzing Information (data) for some purpose. Researchers use different methods in their research activities. The selection of such method depends on the nature, objectives and population of the study. John. W. Best (1977) says, "Research is a more systematic activity directed towards discovery and the development of an organized body of knowledge" (P-308) Educational researchers generally use methods such as survey research, experimental research, historical research, ethnographic research and comparative research.

HYPOTHESES

1. There is a significant difference in the fluency level between men and women teacher trainees.
2. There is a significant difference in the flexibility level between men and women teacher trainees.
3. There is a significant difference in the originality level between men and women teacher trainees.
4. There is a significant difference in the personal adequacy between men and women teacher trainees.
5. There is a significant difference in the interpersonal adequacy between men and women teacher trainees.
6. There is a significant difference in the social adequacy between men and women teacher trainees.
7. There is a significant difference in the social maturity between men and women teacher trainees.
8. There is a significant difference between teacher trainees studying in Government and Aided Institutions with respect to fluency level.
9. There is a significant difference between teacher trainees studying in Government and Either Institutions with respect to flexibility level.
10. There is a significant difference between teacher trainees studying in Government and Aided Institutions with respect to originality level.
11. There is a significant difference between teacher trainees studying in Government and Aided Institutions with respect to personal adequacy on social maturity.
12. There is a significant difference between teacher trainees studying in Government and Aided Institutions with respect to Interpersonal adequacy on social maturity.

13. There is a significant difference between teacher trainees studying in Government and Aided Institutions with respect to social adequacy on social maturity.
14. There is a significant difference between teacher trainees studying in Government and Aided Institutions with respect to social maturity.
15. There is a significant difference between teacher trainees studying in first year and second year with respect to fluency level on creativity.
16. There is a significant difference between teacher trainees studying in first year and second year with respect to flexibility level on creativity.
17. There is a significant difference between teacher trainees studying in first year and second year with respect to originality level on creativity.
18. There is a significant difference between teacher trainees studying in first year and second year with respect to personal adequacy on social maturity scale.
19. There is a significant difference between teacher trainees studying in first year and second year with respect to interpersonal adequacy on social maturity scale.
20. There is a significant difference between teacher trainees studying in first year and second year with respect to Social adequacy on social maturity scale.
21. There is a significant difference between teacher trainees studying in first year and second year with respect to social maturity scale.
22. There is a significant difference between teacher trainees of the creativity factors based on their father's qualifications.
23. There is a significant difference between teacher trainees of the social maturity based on their father's qualifications.
24. There is a significant difference between teacher trainees of the creativity factors based on their mother's qualifications.

25. There is a significant difference between teacher trainees of the social maturity based on their mother's qualifications.
26. There is a significant difference between teacher trainees of the creativity factors based on their parental income.
27. There is a significant difference between teacher trainees of the social maturity based on their Parental Income.
28. There is significant relationship between creativity dimensions and personal adequacy of teacher trainees.
29. There is significant relationship between creativity dimensions and interpersonal adequacy of teacher trainees.
30. There is significant relationship between creativity dimensions and social adequacy of teacher trainees.
31. There is significant relationship between creativity dimensions and social maturity of teacher trainees.

TOOLS SELECTED FOR THE PRESENT STUDY

The study aims at studying the creative thinking and social maturity of Secondary Grade teacher Trainees. For measuring the investigator had used the Verbal Test for Creative Thinking prepared and standardized by Baqer Mehdi, (1973).

Description of the Verbal Test

The Verbal test of creativity includes four sub tests namely consequences test, unusual test, new relationship test and product improvement test.

Consequences test

The consequences tests consist of three hypothetical situations. A) What would happen if man could fly like birds? B) What would happen if our college had wheels? C) What would happen if man does not have any need for food?

Their subject is required to think as many consequences of these situations as he can and write them under each situation in the space provided. The situations being hypothetical minimize the effects of experiences and also provide the subject with an unlimited opportunity to make responses. The test encourages free play of imagination and originality. An example is given on the test booklet to acquaint the subjects with the nature of the test. The time allowed for the three problems is 4 minutes each.

Unusual Test

This test presents the subjects with the names of three common objects and requires him to write as many novel, interesting and unusual uses of these objects as he may think of. The example given on the test booklet properly acquaints the subjects with the nature of the task. The test measures the subjects ability to retrieve items of information from his personal information in storage. Evidently, it measures also the subjects ability to shift frames of reference to use the environment in an original manner. The time allowed for the three tasks is 5 minutes each.

New-Relationship test

This test presents the subject with three pairs of words apparently different tree and house chair and ladder, air and water and requires him to think and write as many novel relationship as possible between the two objects of each pair in the space provided. The test provides an opportunity for the free play of imagination and originality. The time allowed for each pair of words is 5 minutes.

Product improvement test

In this test; the subject is asked to think of simple wooden toy of horse and suggest addition of new things to it to make it more interesting for the children to play. The time allowed is 6 minutes.

The total time required for administering the test is 48 minutes in addition to the time necessary for giving instruction, passing out test booklets to children and collecting them back.

RELIABILITY OF THE TEST

The test-retest reliabilities of the factor scores and also the

Total score were obtained on a small sample (N-50). Test-retest reliabilities of Factor scores and Total creativity score.

Table 1.

Reliability coefficient of the creativity test

Fluency	Flexibility	Originality
0.945	0.921	0.896

It may be seen that both the factor score and total creativity score reliabilities are considerably high ranging from 0.896 to 0.945. These values are highly satisfactory. The reliability of the total score, which come out to be 927, is again quite high. Inter scorer reliabilities, for the factor scores in one study were found to range from 653 to 981.

VALDITY OF THE TEST

The Validity co-efficient for each factor are given in table. The index of Validity is the square toot of reliability and is given in the table 3.02

Table 2

Fluency	Flexibility	Originality
0.97	0.96	0.95

All correlations are significant beyond .01 levels. The validity coefficient for factor scores and the total creativity score are high enough to place confidence in the use of the test.

POPULATION AND SAMPLE

The study is related to creative thinking of Secondary grade teacher trainees studying in Chennai city.

SAMPLE

225 teacher trainees were taken for the study of which 124 students are from Government teacher training institutes and 101 from Government teacher training institutes. The sampling techniques used were stratified random sampling.

TABLE 3

INSTITUTIONS SELECTED FOR THE STUDY

Sl. No	Name of the Institution	No of sample
1.	DIET at Chennai	124
2.	Christopher Teacher Training Institute, Chennai	101

TABLE 4

DISTRIBUTION OF SAMPLE BASED ON GENDER

GENDER	FREQUENCY	PERCENTAGE
Men	125	55.6
women	100	44.4
Total	225	100

TABLE 5

DISTRIBUTION OF SAMPLE BASED ON TYPE OF MANAGEMENT

MANAGEMENT	FREQUENCY	PERCENTAGE
Government	124	55.6
Aided	101	44.4
Total	225	100

ADMINISTRATION OF THE BEST

The test administer first gets himself acquainted with the test by carefully going through the test booklet, which contains the general, instructions and instructions and instructions for each activity. The timings given for each activity adhered to.

1. The place for administering the test was such that the teacher trainees may work comfortably and without disturbance. The usual setting for the test administration is in the classroom. The pupils were properly motivated to take the test the language used by the administrator in giving institutions to children was as simple as possible so that each one understands what is required of him. The test administrator had a stopwatch nothing the timing for each activity.

PROCEDURE FOR SCORING

As there is no right or wrong response for the test much care has to be exercised at the time of scoring and the use of scoring sheet. Each item is to be scored for fluency, flexibility and originality. The scoring procedure is given below.

(i) Fluency

Fluency is represented by the number of relevant and unrepeated ideas which the tester produces. Relevance is judged to the basis of the appropriateness of the response when considered in relation to the test problem. An unrepeated idea is one which has been expressed only once under a given problem.

(ii) Flexibility

Flexibility is represented by a person's ability to produce ideas, which differ in approach or thought trend. All ideas which fall under one category of though trend are treated as one for purpose of flexibility scoring. Thus is five ideas are produced and all belong to only one category of approach, flexibility will be one but if all the five ideas are based on five different approaches or thought trends, then the flexibility score will be five.

(iii) Originality

Originality is represented by uncommonness of a given response. The uncommon the response the higher the originality werights.

SOCIAL MATURITY SCALE

To study the Social Maturity of secondary grade teacher-trainees the SMS (Social Maturity Scale) designed and Standardized by Dr. Nalini Rao Ph.D was selected and used.

RELIABILITY AND VALIDITY OF THE TEST

In order to establish the reliability of the Social Maturity Scale the odd-even method was used. Pilot study was conducted among fifty secondary grade teacher trainees. The reliability coefficient was computed by using Spearman's formula to be 0.87. The intrinsic validity was found to be 0.93. Hence the Social Maturity Scale was selected for the study.

COLLECTION OF DATA

As planned earlier the Investigator approached the head of the Institutions with the appraisal of the research programme. The social maturity scale was administered to the students in groups in the regular class room situation with the help of the teachers in change of the teacher trainees. The investigator gave the instruction to the teacher trainees so as to ensure better co-operation and get their responses objectively. The time allowed to complete the scale items was one hour.

SCORING

Nearly fifty percent of the items on each sub scale were worded in the Positive direction and the other half were negatively oriented. Thus the positively oriented statements had their "mature" in the disagreement direction. The scale points on the intervals were subsequently scored 4,3,2,1 for all the positive items where the highest score represented the most mature response and the negative items where the highest scored in the reversed order. Among the 90 items the positive statements are 17, 21, 24, 26, 36, 39, 41, 50, 51, 52, 54, 57, 63, 74, 80, 83, 86, 87 and 90. The remaining were the negative statements. The scoring was done according to the scoring key given in the manual.

STATISTICAL TECHNIQUES USED

Research dispends on statistics. When descriptions are quantified they can be analyzed well. Statistical techniques must be familiar with basic statistical procedure, their limitations in usage and the areas of their application. These procedures help to find the estimates of the population. The investigator has planned to use the following statistical techniques for the analysis of data.

Suitable descriptive and inferential statistical techniques were used in the interpretation of the data to draw our more meaningful picture of results from the collected data. In the present study following statistical measures were used.

(a) mean

(b) Standard Deviation

$$SD = \sigma\sqrt{\frac{\sum fd}{N} - \left[\frac{\sum fd}{N}\right]} \; 2$$

(c) Standard error of mean deviation

$$SEMD = \sqrt{\frac{\sigma_2^2}{N_1}1 + \frac{\sigma_2^2}{N_2}}$$

(d) Critical Ratio

$$= \frac{\sum fd}{\sum f} xi$$

(e) Correlation Coefficient (r)

$$C.R. = \frac{N\sum xy - \sum x \sum y}{(N\sum x - (\sum x)^2 (N\sum y - (\sum y)^2}$$

(f) F - ratio

$$F.ratio = \frac{Variancebetweengroup}{Variancewithingroup}$$

CONCLUSTION

This chapter outlines the design of the present study, the procedure followed and the nature of the sample. It describes the hypotheses to be tested, the tool used and the methods of administration and scoring. The method of investigation designed and followed was found to be quite appropriate and effective for the study.

4

Analysis of the Data

INTRODUCTION

According to Wilkinson and Bhandarkar (1987), analysis of data involves a number of closely related operations that are performed with the purpose of summarizing the collected data and organizing these in such a manner that will yield answer to research question or suggest hypotheses or questions if no such questions hypothesis had initiated the study.

This chapter focuses on statistical analysis to test the hypotheses framed in this study and report of the obtained findings in interpreted. The influence of social maturity on creativity was analysed using appropriate statistics. The same was also analysed considering the background variables namely gender, type of the institution, parental education and year of study. The statistical techniques were mean, standard deviation, t-ratio ANOVA and coefficients of correlations were used.

TESTING OF HYPOTHESIS

HYPOTHESIS - 1

There is a significant difference in the fluency level between men and women teacher trainees

TABLE 1

DIFFERENCE BETWEEN FLUENCY LEVEL OF MEN AND WOMEN TEACHER TRAINEES

Creativity	Gender	N	Mean	S.D	S.E.M.	t-ratio	L.S
Fluency	Male	125	16.66	8.860	0.79	1.12	N.S
	Female	100	17.94	8.079	0.81		

INTERPRETATION

From the above table it is observed that the mean scores obtained for the men and women teacher trainees for fluency level of creativity shows that female member scores higher than the male teacher trainees. But it is not statistically proved and hence the empirical hypothesis is not proved.

HYPOTHESIS - 2

There is a significant difference in the flexibility level between men and women teacher trainees

TABLE 2

DIFFERENCE BETWEEN FLEXIBILITY LEVEL OF MEN AND WOMEN TEACHER TRAINEES

Creativity	Gender	N	Mean	S.D	S.E.M.	t-ratio	L.S
Flexibity	Male	125	15.93	8.424	0.75	2.34	0.05
	Female	100	18.35	6.746	0.68		

INTERPREATION

From the above table it is observed that the mean scores obtained for the men and women teacher trainees for flexibility level of creativity shows that female member scores higher than the male teacher trainees. But it neither is no statistically proved that there is a significant difference at 0.05 levels hence the empirical hypothesis is retained.

HYPOTHESIS - 3

There is a significant difference in the originality level between men and women teacher trainees

TABLE 3

DIFFERENCES BETWEEN ORIGINALITY LEVEL OF MEN AND WOMEN TEACHER TRAINEES

Creativity	Gender	N	Mean	S.D	S.E.M.	t-ratio	L.S
Originality	Male	125	18.86	7.326	0.66	2.94	0.01
Female	100	15.85	7.921	0.80			

INTERPREATION

From the above table it is observed that the mean scores obtained for the men and women teacher trainees for fluency level of originality level of creativity shows that female member scores higher than the male teacher trainees. It is also statistically proved to be significant at 0.01 level and hence the empirical hypothesis is retained.

HYPOTHESIS - 4

There is a significant difference in the personal adequacy between men and women teacher trainees

TABLE 4

DIFFERENCES BETWEEN PERSONAL ADEQUANCY OF MEN AND WOMEN TEACHER TRAINEES

Creativity	Gender	N	Mean	S.D	S.E.M.	t-ratio	L.S
Personal	Male	125	98.86	34.44	3.08	1.180	N.S
Adequacy	Female	100	99.72	25.30	2.53		

INTERPREATION

From the above table it is observed that the mean scores obtained for the men and women teacher trainees for the personal adequacy of social ma shows that female member scores higher than the male teacher trainees. But the difference is not significant and hence the empirical hypothesis is rejected.

HYPOTHESIS - 5

There is a significant difference in the interpersonal adequacy between men and women teacher trainees

TABLE 5

DIFFERENCES BETWEEN INTERPERSONAL ADEQUACY OF MEN AND WOMEN TEACHER TRAINEES

Creativity	Gender	N	Mean	S.D	S.E.M.	t-ratio	L.S
Interpersonal Adequacy	Male	125	108.03	28.45	2.54	1.694	N.S
	Female	100	107.53	24.73	2.47		

INTERPREATION

From the above table it is observed that the mean scores obtained for the men and women teacher trainees for the interpersonal adequacy of social maturity shows that female member scores higher than the male teacher trainees. But it is not statistically proved. Hence the empirical hypothesis is rejected.

HYPOTHESIS - 6

There is a significant difference in the social adequacy between men and women teacher trainees

TABLE 6

DIFFERENCES BETWEEN SOCIAL ADEQUACY OF MEN AND WOMEN TEACHER TRAINEES

Creativity	Gender	N	Mean	S.D	S.E.M.	t-ratio	L.S
Social adequacy	Male	125	98.40	28.59	2.55	1.033	N.S
	Female	100	94.17	32.75	3.28		

INTERPREATION

From the above table it is observed that the mean scores obtained for the men and women teacher trainees for Social adequacy of social maturity shows that male member scores higher than the female teacher trainees. It is also statistically not proved and thus the empirical hypothesis is rejected.

HYPOTHESIS - 7

There is a significant difference in the social maturity between men and women teacher trainees

TABLE 7

DIFFERENCES BETWEEN SOCIAL MATURITY OF MEN AND WOMEN TEACHER TRAINEES

Creativity	Gender	N	Mean	S.D	S.E.M.	t-ratio	L.S
Social maturity	Male Female	125 100	305.32 334.42	52.93 80.65	4.73 8.06	1.712	N.S

INTERPREATION

From the above table it is observed that the mean scores obtained for the men and women teacher trainees for fluency level of social maturity shows that female member scores higher than the male teacher trainees. But the difference in means is not significant. Hence the empirical hypothesis is rejected.

HYPOTHESIS - 8

There is a significant difference between teacher trainees studying in Government and Aided Institutions with respect to fluency level.

TABLE 8

DIFFERENCE BETWEEN FLUENCY LEVEL OF TEACHER TRAINEES STUDYING IN GOVERNMENT AND AIDED INSTITUTIONS

Creativity	Institution	N	Mean	S.D	S.E.M.	t-ratio	L.S
Fluency	Government Govt.aided	125 100	17.15 17.34	8.719 8.326	0.167 0.828	0.167	N.S.

INTERPREATION

From the above table it is observed that the mean scores obtained for the fluency level of teacher trainees studying in Government vs. Aided institutions on the creativity show little difference on their fluency level and is not significant at any level. Hence the empirical hypothesis is not proved.

HYPOTHESIS - 9

There is a significant difference between teacher trainees

studying in Government and Aided Institutions with respect to flexibility level.

TABLE 9

DIFFERENCE BETWEEN FLEXIBILITY LEVEL OF TEACHER TRAINEES STUDYING IN GOVERNMENT AND AIDED INSTITUTIONS

Creativity	Institution	N	Mean	S.D	S.E.M.	t-ratio	L.S
Flexibility	Government	125	17.98	7.953	0.714	2.085	0.05
Govt.aided	100	15.81	7.478	0.744			

INTERPREATION

From the above table it is observed that the mean scores obtained for the flexibility level of teacher trainees studying in Government vs. Aided institutions on the creativity show than the teacher trainees studying in the Government institutions have more flexibility level that the aided institutions. The difference is means is found to be significant at 0.05 level and hence the hypothesis is retained.

HYPOTHESIS - 10

There is a significant difference between teacher trainees studying in Government and Aided Institutions with respect to originality level.

TABLE 10

DIFFERENCE BETWEEN ORIGINALITY LEVEL OF TEACHER TRAINEES STUDYING IN GOVERNMENT AND AIDED INSTITUTION

Creativity	Institution	N	Mean	S.D	S.E.M.	t-ratio	L.S
Flexibility	Government	125	16.68	7.712	0.695	1.814	N.S
Govt.aided	100	18.55	7.650	0.761			

INTERPREATION

From the above table it is observed that the mean scores obtained for the originality level of teacher trainees studying in Government vs. Aided institutions on the creativity show difference on their originality level. But it is not statistically proved and hence the empirical hypothesis is not proved.

HYPOTHESIS - 11

There is a significant difference between teacher trainees studying in Government and Aided Institutions with respect to personal adequacy on social maturity.

TABLE 11

DIFFERENCES BETWEEN PERSONAL ADEQUACY OF TEACHER TRAINEES STUDYING IN GOVERNMENT AND AIDED INSTITUTIONS

Creativity	Institution	N	Mean	S.D	S.E.M.	t-ratio	L.S
personal adequacy	Government	125	100.51	25.03	2.331	0.850	NS
	Govt.aided	100	99.54	28.07	2.793		

INTERPREATION

From the above table it is observed that the mean scores obtained for the personal adequacy of teacher trainees studying in Government and Aided institutions on social maturity shows that trainees studying in Government institutions scores higher than the teacher trainees studying in aided institutions. But is not statistically not proved and hence the empirical hypothesis is rejected.

HYPOTHESIS - 12

There is a significant difference between teacher trainees studying in Government and Aided Institutions with respect to interpersonal adequacy on social maturity.

TABLE 12

DIFFERENCE BETWEEN INTERPERSONAL ADEQUACY OF TEACHER TRAINEES STUDYING IN GOVERNMENT AND AIDED INSTITUTIONS

Creativity	Institution	N	Mean	S.D	S.E.M.	t-ratio	L.S
Interpersonal adequacy	Government	125	105.31	27.84	2.500	2.216	0.05
	Govt.aided	100	107.67	23.71	2.310		

INTERPREATION

From the above table it is observed that the mean scores obtained for the interpersonal adequacy of teacher trainees studying in Government and Aided institutions on social maturity shows that trainees studying in Government aided institutions scores higher than the teacher trainees studying in Government institutions. This is statistically proved and found to be significant at 0,05 level and hence the empirical hypothesis is retained.

HYPOTHESIS - 13

There is a significant difference between teacher trainees studying in Government and Aided Institutions with respect to social adequacy on social maturity.

TABLE 13

DIFFERENCE BETWEEN SOCIAL ADEQUACY OF TEACHER TRAINEES STUDYING IN GOVERNMENT AND AIDED INSTITUTIONS

Creativity	Institution	N	Mean	S.D	S.E.M.	t-ratio	L.S
Social adequacy	Government	125	106.50	29.05	2.610	5.821	0.01
	Govt.aided	100	104.27	27.78	2.765		

INTERPREATION

From the above table it is observed that the mean scores obtained for the social adequacy of teacher trainees studying in Government vs. Aided institutions on social maturity shows that trainees studying in Government institutions scores higher than the teacher trainees studying in aided institutions. The difference in means is statistically proved to be significance and hence the empirical hypothesis is retained.

HYPOTHESIS - 14

There is a significant difference between teacher trainees studying in Government and Aided Institutions with respect to social maturity.

TABLE 14

DIFFERENCE BETWEEN SOCIAL MATURITY OF TEACHER TRAINEES STUDYING IN GOVERNMENT AND AIDED INSTITUTIONS

Creativity	Institution	N	Mean	S.D	S.E.M.	t-ratio	L.S
Social maturity	Government	125	312.32	23.59	4.45	2.02	0.05
	Govt.aided	100	318.48	22.05	4.85		

INTERPREATION

From the above table it is observed that the mean scores obtained for the social maturity teacher trainees studying in Government vs. Aided institutions on social maturity shows that trainees studying in Government aided institutions scores higher than the teacher trainees studying in Government institutions. It is statistically not proved and hence the empirical hypothesis is rejected.

HYPOTHESIS - 15

There is a significant difference between teacher trainees studying in first year and second year with respect to fluency level of creativity.

TABLE 15

DIFFERENCE BETWEEN FLUENCY LEVEL OF TEACHER TRAINEES STUDYING FIRST YEAR AND SECOND YEAR

Creativity	Institution	N	Mean	S.D	S.E.M.	t-ratio	L.S
Fluency	I^{st} Year	112	18.62	7.43	0.70	2.45	0.05
	2nd year	113	15.86	9.31	0.87		

INTERPREATION

From the above table it is observed that the mean scores obtained for the first year and second year teacher trainees for fluency level of creativity shows that first year students scores higher than the second year teacher trainees. It is statistically proved and hence the empirical hypothesis is proved.

HYPOTHESIS - 16

There is a significant difference between teacher trainees studying in first year and second year with respect to flexibility level of creativity.

TABLE 16

DIFFERENCES BETWEEN FLEXIBILITY LEVEL OF TEACHER TRAINEES STUDYING FIRST YEAR AND SECOND YEAR

Creativity	Institution	N	Mean	S.D	S.E.M.	t-ratio	L.S
Flexibility	Ist Year	112	16.82	7.81	0.73	0.35	NS
	2nd year	113	17.19	7.81	0.73		

INTERPREATION

From the above table it is observed that the mean scores obtained for the first year and second year teacher trainees for flexibility level of creativity shows that second year students scores higher than the first year teacher trainees. It is statistically not proved and hence the empirical hypothesis is not proved.

HYPOTHESIS - 17

There is a significant difference between teacher trainees studying in first year and second year with respect to originality level on creativity.

TABLE 17

DIFFERENCE BETWEEN ORIGINALITY LEVEL OF TEACHER TRAINEES STUDYING FIRST YEAR AND SECOND YEAR

Creativity	Institution	N	Mean	S.D	S.E.M.	t-ratio	L.S
Originality	Ist Year	112	17.38	7.71	0.72	0.29	N.S
	2nd year	113	17.68	7.77	0.73		

INTERPREATION

From the above table it is observed that the mean scores obtained for the first year and second year teacher trainees for originality level of creativity shows that not much difference between first year and second year teacher trainees. Hence the empirical hypothesis is not proved.

HYPOTHESIS - 18

There is a significant difference between teacher trainees studying in first year and second year with respect to fluency level of creativity.

TABLE 18

DIFFERENCES BETWEEN PERSONAL ADEQUACY OF TEACHER TRAINEES STUDYING FIRST YEAR AND SECOND YEAR

Category	Year	N	Mean	S.D	S.E.M.	t-ratio	L.S
Personal Adequacy	Ist Year	112	103.81	35.15	3.32	0.208	N.S
	2nd year	113	106.25	30.57	3.42		

INTERPREATION

From the above table it is observed that the mean scores obtained for personal adequacy of teacher trainees studying first year and second year on social maturity shows that trainees studying second year scored higher than the teacher trainees studying in first year. It is statistically not paved and hence the empirical hypothesis is rejected.

HYPOTHESIS - 19

There is a significant difference between teacher trainees studying in first year and second year with respect to interpersonal adequacy on social maturity scale.

TABLE 19

DIFFERENCES BETWEEN INTERPERSONAL ADEQUACY OF TEACHER TRAINEES STUDYING FIRST YEAR AND SECOND YEAR

Category	Year	N	Mean	S.D	S.E.M.	t-ratio	L.S
Interpersonal Adequacy	Ist Year	112	123.86	25.16	2.26	1.243	N.S
	2nd year	113	109.60	25.68	2.41		

INTERPREATION

From the above table it is observed that the mean scores obtained for the interpersonal adequacy of teacher trainees studying first year and second year on social maturity shows that trainees studying first year scored higher than the teacher trainees studying in second year. It is statistically proved and hence the empirical hypothesis is rejected.

HYPOTHESIS - 20

There is a significant difference between teacher trainees studying in first year and second year with respect to social adequacy on social maturity scale.

TABLE 20

DIFFERENCES BETWEEN SOCIAL ADEQUACY OF TEACHER TRAINEES STUDYING FIRST YEAR AND SECOND YEAR

Category	Year	N	Mean	S.D	S.E.M.	t-ratio	L.S
Social	Ist Year	112	98.38	32.09	3.03	0.907	N.S
Adequacy	2nd year	113	94.68	28.88	2.72		

INTERPREATION

From the above table it is observed that the mean scores obtained for social adequacy of teacher trainees studying first year and second year on social maturity shows that trainees studying first year scored higher than the teacher trainees studying in second year. It is statistically not proved and hence the empirical hypothesis is rejected.

HYPOTHESIS - 21

There is a significant difference between teacher trainees studying in first year and second year with respect to social maturity scale.

TABLE 21

DIFFERENCES BETWEEN SOCIAL MATURITY OF TEACHER TRAINEES STUDYING FIRST YEAR AND SECOND YEAR

Category	Year	N	Mean	S.D	S.E.M.	t-ratio	L.S
Social	Ist Year	112	309.04	29.39	7.71	0.41	N.S
Maturity	2nd year	113	310.53	25.12	5.76		

INTERPREATION

From the above table it is observed that the mean scores obtained for social maturity of teacher trainees studying first year and second year on social maturity shows that trainees studying first year scored higher than the teacher trainees studying in second year. It is statistically proved and hence the empirical hypothesis is rejected.

HYPOTHESIS -22

There is a significant difference between the teacher trainees of the creativity factors based on their father's qualifications.

The influence of father's qualification on creativity dimensions has been analysed using ANOVA and the findings are presented in the table 4.22

TABLE 22

RESULTS OF ANOVA FOR THE DIMENSION WISE CREATIVITY FACTORS OF SECONDARY GRADE TEACHER TRAINEES AND QUALIFICATIONS OF THEIR FATHER

Category	Sources of Variation	Sun of Squares	Df	Mean square	F	L.S
Fluency	Between	717.283	5			
	Groups within	15568.609	219	71.409		
	Groups Total	16285.982	224	60.612	1.178	N.S
Originality	Between	402.393	5			
	Groups within	12901.446	218	80.479		
	Groups Total	13303.839	223	59.181	1.360	N.S

From the above table, it is observed that the F value is not significant for the creativity test dimensions of the teacher trainees based on their father's qualifications. So the above empirical hypothesis is rejected.

HYPOTHESIS -23

There is a significant difference between the teacher trainees of the creativity factors based on their father's qualifications.

TABLE 23

RESULTS OF ANOVA FOR THE SOCIAL MATURITY OF SECONDARY GRADE TEACHER TRAINEES AND QUALIFICATIONS OF THEIR FATHER

Category	Sources of Variation	Sun of Squares	Df	Mean square	F	L.S
Personal adequacy	Between Groups	64196.322	5			
	within Groups	1647925.4	219	12839.264		
	Total	1712121.7	224	7524.773	1.706	N.S
Interprets adequacy	Between Groups	51813.041	5			
	within Groups	1609758.4	219	10362.608		
	Total	1661571.4	224	7350.495	1.410	N.S
Social adequacy	Between	24621.711	5			
	Groups within	206123.45	219	492.542		
	Groups Total	208586.16	224	941.203	0.523	N.S
Social Maturity	Between Groups	115358.16	5			
	within Groups	3510108.4	219	23071.631		
	Total	3635466.6	224	16027.892	1.439	N.S

INTERPRETATION

From the above table, it is observed that the F value is not significant for the overall social maturity and dimensions of the teacher trainees based on their father's qualifications. So the above empirical hypothesis is rejected.

HYPOTHESIS -24

There is a significant difference between the teacher trainees of the creativity factors based on their mother's qualifications.

TABLE 24

RESULTS OF ANOVA FOR THE DIMENSION WISE CREATIVITY FACTORS OF SECONDARY GRADE TEACHER TRAINEES AND QUALIFICATIONS OF THEIR MOTHER

Category	Sources of Variation	Sun of Squares	Df	Mean square	F	L.S
Fluency	Between Groups	551.936	5			
	within Groups	15734.046	219	110.387		
	Total	16285.982	224	71.845	1.536	N.S
Flexibility	Between Groups	218.524	5			
	within Groups	13412.472	219	43.705		
	Total	13630.996	224	61.244	0.714	N.S
Originality	Between Groups	287.130	5			
	within Groups	13016.709	218	57.426		
	Total	13303.839	223	59.710	0.960	N.S

INTERPRETATION

The influence of father's qualification on creativity dimensions has been analysed using ANOVA and the findings are presented in the table 4.24 from the above table, it is observed that the F value is not significant inferring no significant difference between groups with respect to creativity factor.

HYPOTHESIS -25

There is a significant difference between the teacher trainees of the social maturity based on their mother's qualifications.

TABLE 25

RESULTS OF ANOVA FOR THE SOCIAL MATURITY OF SECONDARY GRADE TEACHER TRAINEES AND QUALIFICATIONS OF THEIR MOTHER

Category	Sources of Variation	Sun of Squares	Df	Mean square	F	L.S
Personal adequacy	Between Groups	45566.538	5			
	within Groups	1666555.21	219	9113.308		
	Total	712121.7	224	7609.841	1.198	N.S
Interprets adequacy	Between Groups	31217.820	5			
	within Groups	1661571.4	219	6243.564		
	Total	1630353.6	224	7444.537	0.839	N.S
Social adequacy	Between Groups	3969.280	5			
	within Groups	204616.88	218	793.858		
	Total	208586.16	223	934.324	0.850	N.S

Social Maturity	Between Groups	69632.865	5			
	within Groups	3555833.7	219	13926.573		
	Total	3625466.6	224	16236.684	0.858	N.S

INTERPRETATION

From the above table, it is observed that the F value is not significant for the overall social maturity and dimensions of the teacher trainees based on their mother's qualifications. So the above empirical hypothesis is rejected.

HYPOTHESIS -26

There is a significant difference between the teacher trainees of the creativity factors based on their parental income.

TABLE 26

RESULTS OF ANOVA FOR THE DIMENSION WISE CREATIVITY FACTORS OF SECONDARY GRADE TEACHER TRAINEES AND INCOME OF THE PARENTS

Category	Sources of Variation	Sun of Squares	Df	Mean square	F	L.S
Fluency	Between Groups	25.717	2			
	within Groups	16260.265	222	12.859		
	Total	16285.982	224	73.244	0.176	N.S
Flexibility	Between Groups	29.399	2			
	within Groups	13601.596	222	14.700		
	Total	13630.996	224	61.268	0.240	N.S
Originality	Between Groups	394.534	2			
	within Groups	12909.305	222	58.15		
	Total	13303.839	224	59.39	0.98	N.S

INTERPRETATION

The influence of parental income on creativity dimensions has been analysed using ANOVA and the findings are presented in the table 4.26 from the above table, it is observed that the F value is not significant among the mean creativity test dimensions of the teachers trainees based on their parental income. So the above empirical hypothesis is rejected.

HYPOTHESIS -27

There is a significant difference between the teacher trainees of the social maturity based on their father's qualifications.

TABLE 27

OF ANOVA FOR THE SOCIAL MATURITY OF SECONDARY GRADE TEACHER TRAINEES AND PARENTIAL INCOME

Category	Sources of Variation	Sun of Squares	Df	Mean square	F	L.S
Personal adequacy	Between Groups	11677.170	2			
	within Groups	1700444.5	222	5838.585		
	Total	1712121.7	224	7659.660	1.198	N.S
Interprets adequacy	Between Groups	31217.820	2			
	within Groups	1661571.4	222	9545.868		
	Total	1630353.6	224	7398.557	1.290	N.S
Social adequacy	Between Groups	74.461	2			
	within Groups	208511.70	222	37.230		
	Total	208586.16	224	939.242	0.040	N.S
Social Maturity	Between Groups	56404.893	2			
	within Groups	3569061.7	222	28202.446		
	Total	3625466.6	224	16076.854	1.754	N.S

INTERPRETATION

From the above table, it is observed that the F value is not significant among the mean maturity of the teacher trainees based on their parental income. So the above empirical hypothesis is rejected.

HYPOTHESIS - 28

There is significant relationship between creativity dimension and personal adequacy of teacher trainees.

TABLE 28

CORRELATION COEFFICIENT BETWEEN CREATIVITY DIMENSION AND PERSONAL ADEQUACY OF SECONDARY GRADE TEACHER TRAINEES.

Category	N	r	L.S
Fluency Vs Personal adequacy	225	0.03	N.S
Flexibility Vs Personal adequacy	225	0.02	N.S
Originality Vs Personal adequacy	225	0.04	N.S

INTERPRETATION

The coefficient of the correlation given in the Table 4.28 indicates no significant relation between creativity factors and personal adequacy of secondary grade teacher trainees. So the above empirical hypothesis is not accepted.

HYPOTHESIS - 29

There is significant relationship between creativity dimension and inter personal adequacy of teacher trainees.

TABLE 29

CORRELATION COEFFICIENT BETWEEN CREATIVITY DIMENSION AND INTERPERSONAL ADEQUACY OF SECONDARY GRADE TEACHER TRAINEES

Category	N	r	L.S
Fluency Vs Personal adequacy	225	0.07	N.S
Flexibility Vs Personal adequacy	225	0.01	N.S
Originality Vs Personal adequacy	225	0.01	N.S

INTERPRETATION

The coefficient of the correlation given in the Table 4.29 indicates no significant relation between creativity factors and interpersonal adequacy of secondary grade teacher trainees. So the above empirical hypothesis is not accepted.

HYPOTHESIS - 30

There is significant relationship between creativity dimension and social adequacy of teacher trainees.

TABLE 30

CORRELATION COEFFICIENT BETWEEN CREATIVITY DIMENSION AND SOCIAL ADEQUACY OF SECONDARY GRADE TEACHER TRAINEES

Category	N	r	L.S
Fluency Vs Personal adequacy	225	0.37	N.S
Flexibility Vs Personal adequacy	225	0.02	N.S
Originality Vs Personal adequacy	225	0.06	N.S

INTERPRETATION

The coefficient of the correlation given in the Table 4.30 indicates no significant relation between creativity factors and social adequacy of secondary grade teacher trainees. So the above empirical hypothesis is not accepted.

HYPOTHESIS - 31

There is significant relationship between creativity dimension and social maturity of teacher trainees.

TABLE 31

CORRELATION COEFFICIENT BETWEEN CREATIVITY DIMENSION AND SOCIAL MATURITY OF SECONDARY GRADE TEACHER TRAINEES

Category	N	r	L.S
Fluency Vs Personal adequacy	225	0.08	N.S
Flexibility Vs Personal adequacy	225	0.02	N.S
Originality Vs Personal adequacy	225	0.04	N.S

INTERPRETATION

The coefficient of the correlation given in the Table 4.31 indicates no significant relation between creativity factors and social maturity of secondary grade teacher trainees. So the above empirical hypothesis is not accepted.

CONCLUSION

This Chapter Summaries the analysis of data. Testing of hypothesis description and discussion of the table. A brief report of the research study together with the major findings and conclusion along their educational implication has been presented in the succeeding chapter.

5

Summary of Findings and Conclusions

INTRODUCTION

A brief summary of the study stating the problem, the objective, the methodology and the major findings is presented in this chapter. This implication of the study is then discussed, suggesting a few areas for further research.

STATEMENT OF THE PROBLEMS

The problem is titled as CREATIVITY AND SOCIAL MATURITY OF TEACHER TRAINEES.

OBJECTIVES OF THE STUDY

The following were the objectives of the study.

1. To find out the significance of difference in the fluency level of men and women teacher trainees.
2. To find out the significance of difference in the flexibility level of men and women teacher trainees.
3. To find out the significance of difference in the originality level of men of women teacher trainees.

4. To find out the significance of difference in the personal adequacy of men of women teacher trainees.
5. To find out the significance of difference in the interpersonal adequacy of men of women teacher trainees.
6. To find out the significance of difference in the social adequacy of men of women teacher trainees.
7. To find out the significance of difference in the social maturity of men of women teacher trainees.
8. To find out the significance of difference between teacher trainees studying in Government and Government Aided institutions with respect to fluency level.
9. To find out the significance of difference between teacher trainees studying in Government and Government Aided institutions with respect to flexibility level.
10. To find out the significance of difference between teacher trainees studying in Government and Government Aided institutions with respect to originality level.
11. To find out the significance of difference between teacher trainees studying in Government and Government Aided institutions with respect to personal adequacy in social maturity.
12. To find out the significance of difference between teacher trainees studying in Government and Government Aided institutions with respect to Interpersonal adequacy in social maturity.
13. To find out the significance of difference between teacher trainees studying in Government and Government Aided institutions with respect to social adequacy in social maturity.
14. To find out the significance of difference between teacher trainees studying in Government and Government Aided institutions with respect to overall social maturity.
15. To find out the significance of difference between teacher trainees studying in Government and Government Aided institutions with respect to fluency level in creativity.

16. To find out the significance of difference between teacher trainees studying in first year and second year with respect to flexibility level in creativity.
17. To find out the significance of difference between teacher trainees studying in first year and second year with respect to originality level in creativity.
18. To find out the significance of difference between teacher trainees studying in first year and second year with respect to personal adequacy in the social maturity scale.
19. To find out the significance of difference between teacher trainees studying in first year and second year with respect to interpersonal adequacy in the social maturity scale.
20. To find out the significance of difference between teacher trainees studying in first year and second year with respect to social adequacy in the social maturity scale.
21. To find out the significance of difference between teacher trainees studying in first year and second year with respect to overall social maturity.
22. To find out the significance of difference between the teacher trainees in the creativity factors based on their father's qualifications.
23. To find out the significance of difference between the teacher trainees in social maturity based on their father's qualifications.
24. To find out the significance of difference between the teacher trainees in the creativity factors based on their mother's qualifications.
25. To find out the significance of difference between the teacher trainees in the social maturity based on their mother's qualifications.
26. To find out the significance of difference between the teacher trainees in the creativity factors based on their parental income.
27. To find out the significance of difference between the teacher trainees in the social maturity based on their parental income.

28. To find out the relationship between creativity dimensions and personal adequacy of teacher trainees.
29. To find out the relationship between creativity dimensions and interpersonal adequacy of teacher trainees.
30. To find out the relationship between creativity dimensions and social adequacy of teacher trainees.
31. To find out the relationship between creativity dimensions and social maturity of teacher trainees.

HYPOTHESES OF THE STUDY

1. There is a significant difference in the fluency level between men and women teacher trainees.
2. There is a significant difference in the flexibility level between men and women teacher trainees.
3. There is a significant difference in the originality level between men and women teacher trainees.
4. There is a significant difference in the personal adequacy between men and women teacher trainees.
5. There is a significant difference in the interpersonal between men and women teacher trainees.
6. There is a significant difference in the social adequacy between men and women teacher trainees.
7. There is a significant difference in the social maturity between men and women teacher trainees.
8. There is a significant difference between teacher trainees studying in Government and Aided Institutions with respect to fluency level.
9. There is a significant difference between teacher trainees studying in Government and Aided Institutions with respect to flexibility level.
10. There is a significant difference between teacher trainees studying in Government and Aided Institutions with respect to originality level.
11. There is a significant difference between teacher trainees studying in Government and Aided Institutions with respect to personal adequacy on social maturity.

12. There is a significant difference between teacher trainees studying in Government and Aided Institutions with respect to Interpersonal adequacy on social maturity.
13. There is a significant difference between teacher trainees studying in Government and Aided Institutions with respect to social adequacy on social maturity.
14. There is a significant difference between teacher trainees studying in Government and Aided Institutions with respect to social maturity.
15. There is a significant difference between teacher trainees studying in first year and second year with respect to fluency level on creativity.
16. There is a significant difference between teacher trainees studying in first year and second year with respect to flexibility level on creativity.
17. There is a significant difference between teacher trainees studying in first year and second year with respect to originality level on creativity.
18. There is a significant difference between teacher trainees studying in first year and second year with respect to personal adequacy on social maturity scale.
19. There is a significant difference between teacher trainees studying in first year and second year with respect to interpersonal adequacy on social maturity scale.
20. There is a significant difference between teacher trainees studying in first year and second year with respect to Social adequacy on social maturity scale.
21. There is a significant difference between teacher trainees studying in first year and second year with respect to social maturity scale.
22. There is a significant difference between teacher trainees of the creativity factors based on their father's qualifications.
23. There is a significant difference between teacher trainees of the social maturity based on their father's qualifications.

24. There is a significant difference between teacher trainees of the creativity factors based on their mother's qualifications.
25. There is a significant difference between teacher trainees of the social maturity based on their mother's qualifications.
26. There is a significant difference between teacher trainees of the creativity factors based on their parental income.
27. There is a significant difference between teacher trainees of the social maturity based on their father's qualifications.
28. There is significant relationship between creativity dimensions and personal adequacy of teacher trainees.
29. There is significant relationship between creativity dimensions and interpersonal adequacy of teacher trainees.
30. There is significant relationship between creativity dimensions and social adequacy of teacher trainees.
31. There is significant relationship between creativity dimensions and social maturity of teacher trainees.

TOOLS USED IN THIS STUDY

In order to verify the hypotheses the following tools have been used.

1. Creativity test by Baquer Mehid
2. Rao's Social Maturity Scale.

The Sampling technique used was Staffed Random Sampling. The study was conducted among 225 secondary grade teacher trainees drawn from different Training Institutes.

MAJOR FINDINGS

1. The mean scores obtained for the men and women teacher trainees for fluency level of creativity shows those female members scores higher than the male teacher trainees.
2. The mean scores obtained for the men and women teacher trainees for flexibility level of creativity shows those female members scores higher than the male teacher trainees and it is statistically proved and thus the hypothesis is retained.

3. It was found that a significant difference occurred in the originality of men and women teacher trainees.
4. The mean scores obtained for the men and women teacher trainees for personal adequacy of social maturity shows that women teacher trainees are having more personal adequacy than the men teacher trainees.
5. For the interpersonal adequacy of social maturity showed that male members scores higher than the female teacher trainees.
6. It was found that there was no significant difference in the social adequacy of men and women teacher trainees.
7. There was no significant difference in the social maturity of men and women teacher trainees.
8. It was found that there was no significant difference in the fluency and originality level of teacher trainees studying in Government and Government Aided Institutes. In the case of flexibility level significant difference was found among the teacher trainees.
9. Significant differences were found between teacher trainees studying Government and Government Aided Secondary Grade Training Institutes on their social adequacy, personal adequacy, interpersonal and social maturity.
10. It was found that there was no significant difference in the flexibility and originality level of teacher trainees studying first year and second year teacher trainees. In the case of fluency level significant difference was found among the teacher trainees.
11. In the case of social maturity and its dimensions significant differences were not found between the teacher trainees studying first year and second year courses.
12. Parental qualifications, income of the parents, and their educational qualifications have no significant influence on the creativity and social maturity of the teacher trainees.

EDUCATIONAL IMPLICATIONS

One of the objectives of carrying out this research is to arrive at specific conclusions. Conclusions are essentially an important outcome of research and are derived from the data analysis and interpretations. The aim of the present study was to study creativity and social maturity of secondary grade teacher trainees.

When analyzing creativity is, it is helpful to consider creativity as something that is necessary for the discovery of creative solutions to problems. Solving problems is not just a scientific or engineering activity, even educationists are commissioned to express a concept or an idea in a certain way.

Following the theme of creative solutions to problems, what makes one solution creative and another simply ordinary. It seems that it is often to context within which solution is offered that establishes creativity. This means that creativity is not simple simply a mental process there may be little to distinguish creativity from expertise. Creative solutions are very much need for the problem active society. It is very essential for the teacher trainees to train them to have a creative solution in the classrooms. So social maturity is very much needed for the teacher trainees also.

In this study it was found that the teacher trainees are not much different in their social maturity as well as their creativity level based on their gender, type of management of the institutions and their year of study also. Parental qualifications and parental income may not show significant influence on the creativity dimensions and social maturity and its dimensions. The teacher training institutions make a significant role in including the creativity and social maturity the teacher trainees.

The institutions should chalks out programmes to nourish creativity among the teacher trainees. The flexible curriculum the democratic administration through councils an committees, scientific and recreational hobbies, dramatics, writing competitions painting debates, cultural activities not only develop their creativity but also make them to be a well matured person. The trainees become a good creative teacher. A creative teacher is sensitive to the problems arising either in the classrooms or in the school and has got the capacity to suggest more than one solution to solve these problems.

SUGGESTIONS FOR FURTHER RESEARCH

This study confines itself to the survey of secondary grade teacher trainees in the Chennai Educational district only and therefore cannot claim to have comprehensiveness nor can its conclusions be claimed to be universally valid. This is however a beginning and the results hold promise to lead a more comprehensive and in depth investigation into the interaction between creativity and social maturity.

For more universal and unbiased results, this study may be replicated with the following modifications.

1. Relationship between the creativity and learning styles of the teacher trainees can be undertaken.
2. Relationship between creativity, Hemisphericity and achievement motivation can be analysed.
3. Relationship between creativity, social intelligence and personality types can be studied.

6

Societal Needs in Higher Education

Introduction

Thousands of graduates are coming out from different Indian Universities every year. All these graduates have no practical knowledge and lacks self-confidence and even they cannot make their earning activity independently. The present higher education system fails to adopt a long-term vision and will result in increasing poverty, unemployment, migration and outdated thinking patterns. The quality of the higher education should be made responsive to the requirements of changed or changing society. Now days the society is very much dynamic, the present society has no longer require muscle power rather, it requires brainpower instead of clinging to fixed ideas and rigid thinking patterns, the system of higher education can be changed in to new dimensions. In an increasingly global and complex world, education Curriculum should be revised to concentrate on the needs of each society and personal growth of an individual in an action-oriented approach and not theoretical oriented approach.

Educational institutions and government should be socially responsible to make revolutionary changes in the present curriculum. Whatever they learn should be directly useful in their practical life. Whatever is not useful in the practical life should be eliminated. The more emphasis should be on vocational education. While devising the curriculum, the realistic situation of our country and the requirements of industry should be borne in our mind that the purpose of this paper is to contribute to the on-going discussion on the implications of societal needs and maintaining quality in higher education. This paper intends to identify gap between societal needs and quality in higher education today. It also discusses the opportunities and challenges posed by society to higher education. The aim of this paper is to discuss appropriate policies and strategies to improve the quality of higher education to meet the societal needs.

Higher Education

Higher education includes all types of studies, training or training for research at the post-secondary level provided by universities or other educational establishments that are approved as institutions of higher education by the competent State authorities Higher Education is the important factor of long-term development and it aims at a multidimensional and anticipatory modeling of the human factor. The higher education system must be preserved and enhanced according to the requirements of the knowledge-based society evolution.

There has been a phenomenal expansion of higher education in India in the last few decades as is evident from the enormous increase in the number of universities, colleges and students. But there has been decline in the quality of higher education. Our system of higher education is faced today with the challenge of managing quality assurance.

Quality education

Quality education may be defined as that which transforms the consciousness of a person and leads him from darkness to light. It does so by instilling the following four capabilities in an efficient, effective and excellent manner:

- To make think logically, analytically, critically and laterally.
- To prepare for an honorable living, i.e. employability by learning occupational Skills and work experience.
- To realize one's potential for self-development in terms of physical, Emotional, intellectual, artistic and moral attainment through educational experience.
- To acquire a discriminatory capability to appreciate and absorb the emerging values of our times such as concern for ecology, equality, civility, harmony and cultural pluralism.

Quality and Excellence

In order to impart quality education, our education system itself has to acquire the following five quality pre-requisites:

- Quality syllabus
- Quality faculty
- Quality teaching and evaluation,
- Quality research
- Quality character.

Quality syllabus and faculty

Quality syllabus means regular updating and up gradation of advanced theoretical and experimental thrust, credibility of content, interdisciplinary orientation, sensitivity to emerging intellectual developments and social sensibilities, and especially for self and social development. Some of the essential characteristics of quality faculty include their academic and research eminence, intellectual competence as measured by command over the subject, ability to build an argument in a coherent manner, communicative competence as reflected in clarity of thought and expression as signified by reflective character of teaching.

Quality teaching and evaluation

The important indicators of quality teaching and evaluation are mainly teacher-student ratio, modes of teaching, its interactive and participatory character, innovative teaching methods, regularity of classes, responsibility to completion of syllabus, students interest to attend classes without compulsion of attendance, positive feedback by students, affectivity in teacher-student relationship, regular and continuous assessment, objectivity, impartiality and transparency in evaluation.

Quality research and character

The quality of research can be measured in terms of breaking a new ground, generating a paradigm shift, research publications, acknowledgement by way of frequency of certification, awards of honors, quality of research guidance and projects, etc. The quality of character and outlook of faculty is as important as is the quality of teaching In fact, this constitutes the foundation of quality education. This is so particularly because of the newly recognized role of education as an agency of social change. In this context, the measures of socially relevant quality education are such social sensibilities of faculty as egalitarian, ecological, civil, pluralistic, etc., apart from integrity of character.

Quality in higher education is a multidimensional concept, which should embrace all its functions, and activities: teaching and academic programmes, research and scholarship, staffing, students, buildings, facilities, equipment, services to the community and the academic environment. Internal self-evaluation and external review should be conducted openly by independent specialists, if possible with international expertise, are vital for enhancing quality

Present Scenario of Higher Education in India

India educates approximately 10 per cent of its young people in higher education compared with more than half in the major industrialized countries and 15 per cent in China. India has a massive system of higher education. In spite of having a massive system of higher education, only 7 percent youth of the relevant age group of 17 to 24 years is receiving higher education as compared to France (50%), U.S.A (81%) and Canada (99.8%). At the same time the system has been failed to cater to the heterogeneity of the society.

In India only few of the best universities have some excellent departments and centers, and there are a small number of outstanding undergraduate colleges. The University Grants Commission's recent major support of five universities to build on their recognized strength is a step toward recognizing a differentiated academic system-and fostering excellence. At present, the world-class institutions are mainly limited to the Indian Institutes of Technology (IITs), the Indian Institutes of Management (IIMs) and perhaps a few others such as the All India Institute of Medical Sciences and the Tata Institute of Fundamental Research

Promoting Excellence

In India the UGC has identified only 9 universities and 97 colleges with potential for excellence, and they constitute about 6% of the total universities and 2% of the colleges. Beside about 500 Department, centers and about 12 centers have been identified with potential for excellence... The present evidence shows that a vast number of colleges/state university sectors are of low to medium quality by NAAC measure. Therefore, there is an urgent need to improve the physical and academic infrastructure of these institutions. This calls for a "Revival of college and state university sector". In India only limited number of universities, departments and collages has potential for excellence because most of the university and college education has suffered from the lack of adequate academic and physical infrastructure.

Measurement of Excellence in fulfillment of societal needs

In India only few people are thinking creatively about higher education. There is no field of higher education research. Government as well as academic leaders seems content to do the "same old system of doing things." Academic institutions and systems have become large and complex. These institutions need good data, careful analysis, and creative ideas to make revolutionary changes. In China, more than two-dozen higher education research centers, and several government agencies are involved in higher education policy

Most of the Indians colleges and universities are under-funded, ungovernable institutions. Under-investment in libraries, information technology, laboratories and classrooms makes it very difficult to provide top-quality education. The rises in the number of part-time teachers and the freeze on new full-time appointments in many places have affected morale in the academic profession. In India, quality of higher education is faced with great challenges and difficulties related to financing, equity of conditions at access into and during the course of studies, improved staff development, skilled based training, enhancement and presentation of quality in teaching, research and Service, relevance of programmes, employability of graduates. At the same time higher education is being challenged by new opportunities relating to technologies that are improving the ways in which knowledge can be produced, managed, disseminated, accessed and controlled. Equitable access to these technologies should be ensured at all levels of education systems.

In the current context, contemporary higher education is subject today to three important forces that pressure it into changing: globalization, communication and information technology, and competition for resources and students. When deciding upon any development strategy for a education, these three forces have to be taken into consideration and have to be strongly related to the increase of individual demand for higher education in the context of changing society

Transformation in the higher education system to suit societal needs

The University Education Report had set goals for development of higher education in the country. While articulating these goals Radakrishnan Commission on University Education, 1948-49 put it in following words: "The most important and urgent reform needed in education is to transform it, to endeavor to relate it to the life, needs and aspirations of the people and thereby make it the powerful instrument of social, economic and cultural transformation necessary for the realization of the national Goals. For this purpose, education should be developed so as to increase productivity, achieve social and national integration, accelerate the process of modernization and cultivate social, moral and spiritual values."

The primary objectives of an educational system meant to bring its contribution to the development of a knowledge–based society Our education strategy should be based on the concept of change by means of sustainable development, focused on intellectual creativity – a feature that plays an essential role in the transition toward a new model of society and to complying with the requirements of an information-based, intensively cultural society. The strategy of building and improving human resources constitutes a starting point for a modernization policy of education. The educational policies we are going to implement have as the most important objective education itself, and the involvement of all essential actors in the educational process.

Index